A User Guide to The
UNCONSCIOUS MIND

A User Guide to The
UNCONSCIOUS MIND

by Tatiana Lukyanova

atmosphere press

TABLE OF CONTENTS

*For my beloved daughters, Anastasia and Alexandra.
Thank you for all the love, support, and challenges.*

INTRODUCTION

I've written this book for you.

I've translated years of studies, analysis, and scientific research into simple words and stories that will lead you through the pathways of your unconscious mind and bring you to a better understanding of who you are and why you are that way. I believe that this will help you to understand yourself, achieve your goals, and become a happy and balanced person.

I hope that this knowledge will expand your inner world and guide you through your day-to-day life. I believe it will give you greater freedom of choice. That freedom comes with powerful knowledge and the responsibility to use it wisely.

And that is why I've written this book for you—and for your family, friends, colleagues, and any other person who interacts with you. I hope that they will appreciate the kindness and empathy that you may pick up from these chapters.

How to Read This Book

I recommend you read no more than one chapter per day. I suggest you take the opportunity to process the information and reflect on it. Let it assimilate before you go to the next topic.

I encourage you to not skip exercises. This book was designed primarily to help you experience all the theories that are discussed and explained to ensure a thorough understanding.

This book is titled *A User Guide to the Unconscious Mind*, and this is precisely what it represents. Imagine that you are opening a door and staying on the threshold, observing what is inside your own mind. That perspective allows you to see cues to what is happening in the minds of others. This book presents a useful overview of our unconscious mind and provides you with tools to proceed in depth, in any direction you wish.

It all starts with awareness: of what is there, what is possible, what is challenging, and why you react and behave in a certain way.

*This book does not cover personality disorders such as sociopathy, narcissism, nor does it cover developmental disorders such as autism and Asperger syndrome, which may influence the way people perceive, recognize, and experience emotions.

CHAPTER 1
EMOTIONS, DEFINED

It seems like we are all supposed to know what emotions are. We intuitively feel suspicious, on high alert when someone shows emotional bluntness or has what seems to us to be an inadequate emotional reaction. We understand what it means when one says, "Oh, it was such an emotional moment," or "Please, don't be so emotional about it."

It seems obvious that emotions have something to do with the way we feel in a particular moment. At the same time, the way we feel in a specific moment has something to do with our perception of the reality.

When you feel happy, everything around you seems cheerful: The sun is brighter, the grass is greener, and people are smiley.

On the other hand, if you are frightened because you have to go through a dark street late at night, everything seems terrifying: The moonlight is ominous, the sounds are threatening, and the steps are exceptionally loud.

The way we perceive the world in a given moment can reveal a lot about our emotional state. I wish I had the ability to know how you are today. Is it morning or evening time when you have picked up this book and decided to follow the white rabbit of my story? Did you sleep well? Did you have a hard day?

Unfortunately, I don't know, and I can't ask you, but we

can play a game.

Think about rain and how it makes you feel. Take your time and if you want, write down your reaction or draw it here:

Now let's see: Did you envision a melancholy autumn whispering about sunshine that is gone? Maybe a scary thunderstorm with flashes of lightning? Is your reaction/vision full of power, like in the battlefields of *Pirates of the Caribbean* or *Lord of the Rings*? I wonder whether perhaps the scene is romantic, like in *Breakfast at Tiffany's* or *The Notebook*, or joyful, like in *Singin' in the Rain?*

Whatever your answer, it reveals a lot about your current emotional state and your emotional memory. Try to reflect and answer to yourself: Why does your rain look this way today?

Why would a single natural phenomenon like rain elicit a diverse range of descriptions from different people? The answer is emotions. They are in charge of how we feel, how we perceive reality, and what events and associations are most strongly imprinted in memory.

While we all have an intuitive understanding of the

term, when we try to give a definition of emotions, it suddenly eludes us like the words of a song we used to know a long time ago. It becomes blurry and abstract.

What defines an emotion? What is common between anger and sadness, happiness and frustration, fear and woe, joy and revulsion, contempt and surprise, disgust and amazement?

Now, let's try this out: take a pen and write down your definition of emotions. Think about the questions below as you answer, and try to summarize your responses to them in your definition:

- What do emotions mean in your life?
- How attentive are you to your emotional state?
- Why and how do you become emotional?
- How does it feel?
- How do you recognize emotions in others?

I hope you didn't skip through it and instead took the time to think of emotions and write down your definition. Was it easy or difficult? Are you satisfied with what you came up with or does it feel like something is missing?

If you have found it difficult, you are not alone.

Psychologists, psychiatrists, and neurologists are still debating the definition of emotions.

Let's look at one definition given by Antonio Damasio, one of the leading neuroscientists in the world:

"A specific and consistent collection of physiological responses triggered by certain brain systems when [an] organism represents certain objects or situations."
Antonio Damasio (2002)

We are used to connecting emotions to something intuitive, subtle, and elusive. It must be a strange realization to acknowledge that they have a strong physiological component.

Now compare Damasio's definition to one given by Paul Ekman, one of the leading psychologists in the area of emotions and their relation to facial expressions:

"A process, a particular kind of automatic appraisal influenced by our evolutionary and personal past, in which we sense that something important to our welfare is occurring, and a set of psychological changes and emotional behaviors begins to deal with the situation."
Paul Ekman (2007)

Sounds way more personal, doesn't it?

Nevertheless, both definitions agree on one thing: Our emotions, once activated, take control of our reactions, perception of the world, actions, and communication with each other. Moreover (and it will become more and more evident as you proceed through this book), our capacity to control our emotions is much smaller than we used to think.

Charles Darwin describes an excellent example of this in his book *Expression of Emotions in Man and Animals*. Darwin puts his face close to the thick glass of an aquarium with a dangerous snake—a puff adder—determined to remain still even if the snake attempts to strike. Nevertheless, as soon as the snake attacks toward the glass, Darwin jumps back. We can be sure that it would be possible to recognize fear on his face.

Emotions developed as a sort of shortcut between our interaction with the world and our brain's reaction to it. As in the example with Darwin and the puff adder, an emotion like fear will take control of our actions as soon as our brain identifies a threat. Ekman, the psychologist, calls this unconscious and uncontrollable impulse *automatic appraisal*.

Emotions are rapid—they fire up quickly and fade out within minutes or even seconds, unless the environment keeps offering a trigger. That is what separates emotions from moods. Moods last longer; they can stay with us for a few days. It's possible to say that moods resemble a slight and continuous emotional state and make us more vulnerable to corresponding triggers. If one is in an irritable mood, anger will most likely fire up faster and stronger, while for someone in a happy or joyful state, it will be more difficult for anger to break through.

If a mood stays with us too long, it may become a personal trait. For example, somebody who has a tendency to sadness may be known as a melancholic person, while someone who is always afraid might be perceived as timid. While we all have emotions and moods, only a few of us carry emotional traits. We all have moments of feeling blue, but only a few of us can be described as a melancholy person. Even if we all can get very angry or irritable all day, very few of us can be described as hostile. If the trait goes up to its extreme, it may become a psychological disorder.

Emotion	Mood	Trait	Disorder
Anger	Irritable	Hostility	Violence
Fear	Alarmed	Timidity	Phobia/ Anxiety
Disgust	Picky	Squeamishness	Obsessive-Compulsive Disorder
Contempt	Chuffed	Snobbery Arrogance	Narcissism
Sadness	Blue	Melancholy	Depression
Happiness	Contented	Optimism	Mania, Risk-taker

Let's look at how these classifications apply in practice. Look at the list of words. Select those that you think do *not* represent emotions. Also, mark those that you have experienced at least once in the past month.

Livid	Annoyed	Thrilled	Peeved
Frightened	Flabbergasted	Gloomy	Joyful
Scared	Petrified	Glad	Dejected
Resentful	Terrified	Afraid	Amazed
Happy	Hate	Jealousy	Distraught

Miserable	Astounded	Enthusiastic	Panicky
Stunned	Pleased	Shocked	Surprised
Delighted	Worried	Unhappy	Sad
Contemptuous	Derisive	Love	Arrogant
Glum	Disgusted	Condescend-ing	Guilt
Revolted	Repugnant	Repulsed	Sickened
Supercilious	Astonished	Disdainful	Smug
Shame	Nauseous	Angry	Furious

Let's analyze the words that don't represent emotions:

LOVE: A sophisticated feeling related to attachment and commitment within which one can experience many various emotions that are always related to a target of love: romantic love, parental love, or love toward a pet.

HATE: As complicated as love, and usually directed at a person or group and accompanied by anger, disgust, contempt. It can even develop into a hostile trait. It can be quite toxic for a person experiencing it, and can be released with forgiveness, empathy, and compassion.

JEALOUSY: Seems to be strongly related to the individual characteristics of a person who is experiencing it and their circumstances.

SHAME and GUILT: Besides showing the same signals as emotions from the sadness family, these deserve a closer look and will be discussed in Chapter 7.

There are also emotions that are not yet well understood and investigated, and do not have known reliable signals, such as envy and embarrassment.

Meanwhile, because of our shared evolutionary history, many other emotions can be grouped thematically, while variations within a theme are a result of social experiences.

Angry	Frightened	Happy	Sad
Furious	Scared	Ecstatic	Glum
Livid	Afraid	Thrilled	Dejected
Annoyed	Petrified	Joyful	Miserable
Peeved	Terrified	Glad	Gloomy
Resentful	Worried	Pleased	Unhappy
	Panicky	Delighted	Distraught
Surprised	**Contempt-uous**	**Disgusted**	
Flabber-gasted	Derisive	Nauseous	
Amazed	Condescending	Offended	
Astonished	Supercilious	Repulsed	
Astounded	Arrogant	Revolted	
Shocked	Smug	Sickened	
Stunned	Disdainful	Repugnant	

Some other emotional states represent a blend of multiple emotions; for example, frustration can derive from a blend of anger and sadness.

Besides physiological markers such as heart rate, blood pressure, voice pitch, and the like, the seven emotions that now are called universal have distinct facial expressions that help us recognize the emotional state of another person. When we do not trust a person but fail to explain the reasons behind that, most likely our brain is registering discrepancies between their words, posture, facial expressions, and voice. If we are missing theoretical knowledge on how to interpret this information, our brain is still processing it on an unconscious level. This is what we usually call "intuition." Moreover, our own emotional state has a crucial influence on our way of receiving and perceiving verbal and nonverbal information while communicating with others.

SUMMARY:

Emotions occur in response to a stimulus, and they are:
- Rapid,
- Coordinated and organized, and have
- Reliable signals (i.e., physiological changes and expressions)

The function of emotions:
- To motivate behavior—a fast, unconscious reaction to a stimulus
- To facilitate communication of nonverbalized information

CHAPTER 2
EMOTIONS: REASONS AND MECHANISMS

In the previous chapter, we discussed different definitions of emotions and concluded that they have crucial importance in our life and especially in interpersonal communication. Now, get ready to go through the most complicated, but also the most important, chapter of the book.

How do emotions emerge? It is always in reaction to a particular trigger.

The most apparent trigger is an event. For example, getting a bad mark at school can be upsetting or scary if one expects punishment; not getting a well-deserved promotion can make one angry and/or sad; finding rotten food in the fridge can make one feel disgusted; waking up to a sunny day can make one feel happy; receiving unexpected news can make one feel surprised.

We can also trigger an emotion by remembering an event that happened to us in the past. Recalling a favorite team's loss in a championship, misplacing a favorite object, or the loss of a loved one can make one feel sad again. Similarly, if you tell a friend that someone has mistreated you, you most likely will experience a feeling of anger akin to what you felt during the original event.

On the other hand, pleasant memories can make us feel happy and elevate our mood. Spending time with best friends, walking along the beach, receiving a reward from people who matter to us—we all have these private islands of joy in the land of our memories, and they seem to get better with time.

Our imagination can also trigger emotions; visualizing our fears or dreaming about holidays will launch the same physiological and psychological responses. Imagination can be boosted by reading or tricked by watching movies or news, and will fire up corresponding emotions as well.

Thus, whenever something is happening to us, whenever we are dreaming, thinking, or talking about situations and events, all of it can launch emotional responses and influence our perception of objective reality.

Research suggests that whenever we are able to recreate the physiological conditions that correspond to a particular emotion, we will start to feel that emotion. Thus, when you hear that smiling often makes you happier, it is actually true, insofar as you are smiling correctly (see Chapter 4).

Some triggers are universal and have a lengthy evolutionary background, but most of them are personal to each of us and represent a history of events in our life.

According to brain research (LeDoux, 1996), when an emotional trigger is established, new connections are formed among a group of cells in our brain, forming a so-called cell assembly. The set of cell assemblies we collect through our lives is what Paul Ekman calls our *emotion alert database*.

If we want to simplify this definition, we could say that the brain memorizes the trigger along with an emotional action script.

Our unconscious brain continuously scans the

environment for known triggers, at the ready to launch an emotion and an emotional response (which can take the form of a physical action). In many cases, the brain recognizes the trigger correctly and fires the right action. Sometimes it can save our lives, as it will make one immediately and without thinking jump off as the brain registers a snake in the grass. On the other hand, the brain also has a margin for error and will make a person jump away from a rope that resembles the snake, just the same way.

When I was a child, I often stayed with my grandparents. My grandma, as a teenager, lived through World War II and the Siege of Leningrad. People in the city had no connection to the external world for 900 days. They experienced aerial bombardment and had no heating to survive through the winter. Every day my grandma would be starving and would see neighbors, relatives, and friends die of hunger. The fear of ending up without a morsel of food, or of losing a valuable object that potentially could be exchanged for food, stayed with my grandma till the end of her days. As a result of this fear, she would unconsciously hide things. Often, she wouldn't remember it, and then family members would agree that I, the irresponsible child, took it or ate it or lost it. The accusation would usually start with a question: "Did you take such-and-such object?" This episode would repeat in my life, again and again, starting with the same question about various objects. So where did it lead?

This form of the question got into my emotional database as a trigger associated with unfair treatment and false accusation. No matter from whom and in what context, when I would hear this question, I would immediately react with frustration. Naturally, for other people in my surroundings, it came off as an entirely inadequate reaction. In the same way that my grandma was still hiding things while the war was long over, I kept defending myself after there was no accusation.

So here we come to an amazing finding:

There is no evidence that learned triggers can be deleted from our emotion alert database.

That means that once learned, a trigger will stay with us forever and the program associated with it will keep automatically generating emotional impulses. Designed by nature and evolution to ensure fast, unconscious reactions, in many cases this reflex enriches and even saves our lives, but sometimes it can lead us to an unwanted outcome if a trigger is false or outdated.

Many factors influence the strength of the trigger:

- The time of initial onset (The earlier the trigger is learned, the harder it is to weaken it.)
- The initial emotional charge (intensity of an emotion)
- The density of experience (repeated episodes)
- How closely the current event resembles the original situation
- The temperament of the person

If we use my example for comparison, we can see that my trigger was learned quite early on—during childhood. The initial emotional charge was medium. Density can be considered very high since it happened repeatedly over a number of years. Finally, my impulse would manifest more strongly if the question were formulated in the same format and came from an elderly woman.

As soon as we become emotional, psychological and physiological changes start to occur, despite our choice and without instant awareness: facial expression, voice, autonomic nervous system activity, related memories, expectations, and, finally, behavioral patterns.

It takes only a fraction of a second for our facial expression to change in accordance with an experienced emotion. It can be assumed that before human speech developed, our facial expressions and body language were our primary communication tools. Even nowadays, as soon as we register fear on somebody's face, we become alerted and unconsciously begin to examine our environment for the source of possible danger. This is also the reason why we can never fully hide our real feelings: no matter how much we wish to keep control over our emotions, corresponding facial expressions will still flash on the face, because they happen faster than we can control. Paul Ekman introduced the term *micro-expressions* to describe this emotional leakage. His research shows that it takes just about an hour of training for an average person to increase recognition of micro-expressions up to 80–100%. That means that if we learn what clues to look for—in this case facial expressions exclusively—we can identify and associate them with a corresponding emotion incredibly quickly—in a fraction of a second.

Physiological changes corresponding to emotion will kick in after 10–15 seconds. These can include perspiration, breathing rate, heart rate, blood pressure, body temperature, muscular tension, local blood circulation, and dehydration. It is interesting to mention that the polygraph, known as a lie-detecting machine, is based on measuring precisely these physiological aspects of our emotional responses.

To understand more about how emotions work, let's do the following exercise:

Try to remember a recent angry episode. On a scale from 0 to 10, try to think of the situation when your anger reached at least a 6 or 7.

What was it that made you angry? How fast did your anger reach its peak? How long did it take you to calm down? When did you realize that you were angry?

Now, look at the axes below, and try to plot your emotional graph. As an example, I offer you a graph that represented my typical anger pattern, before I started my journey toward emotional awareness. As you can see, it commonly would take me a long time to reach an angry state. That also means that my emotional signals toward the source of my anger would be low and could pass unnoticed. At some point, it would reach a boiling point and jump high up, and I would stay at this position for a relatively long period, after which I would slowly start to calm down.

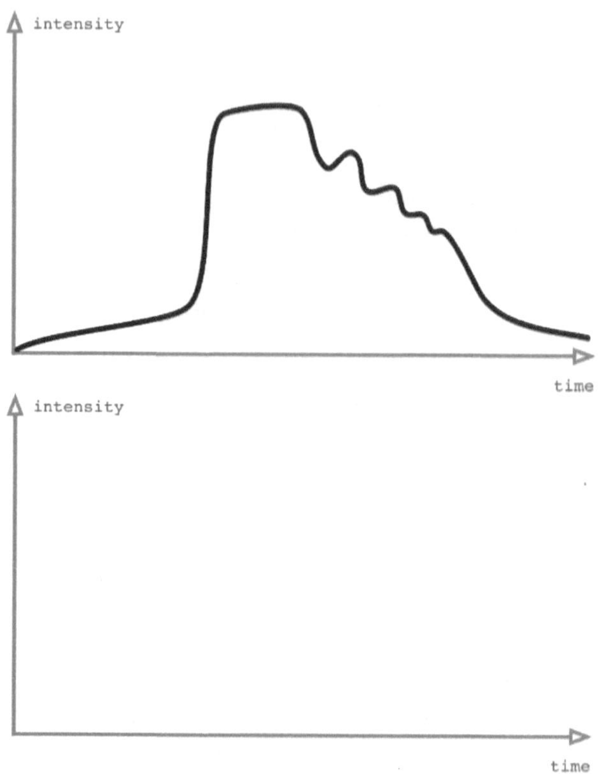

Try to analyze your diagram and think about how your emotional style influences your communication.

According to neurology studies, as soon as we get emotional, the part of the brain responsible for logical thinking becomes inactive, and we are ruled by the amygdala—the integrative center for our emotions.

Here we come to yet another fascinating finding: from the moment an emotional impulse is generated, our brain begins to filter all the external information to feed that emotion in order to keep us focused on the problem. This phenomenon has deep survival roots.

The moment we get scared, our brain begins picking from surrounding information anything that confirms our fear and keeps us focused on the potential threat. Moreover, it interprets any information in such a way that it reinforces that fear.

I'm sure you can recall at least one episode when you got angry with someone, and whatever this person would say only added more fuel to your emotion. The same phenomenon keeps you laughing long after a good joke, even repeating the best part of it.

That interval between an initial emotional impulse and the cognitive processing of a trigger, when our logical thinking is activated again, is called *a refractory period.*

As we discussed earlier, we cannot remove triggers or stop our initial impulse, but we can learn to break the connection between the trigger and the corresponding behavioral script by bringing consciousness to the picture.

Therefore, since I became aware of the "Did you take...?" issue, I still do feel an initial irritation, but I'm able to calm it down immediately by recognizing that the situation and intentions are different.

That is also why we can observe a difference in emotional expressiveness between different people, and even different cultures. As soon as the emotional impulse is generated, it goes through the filter of personal and social norms, commonly called *display rules*, which will be discussed in detail in Chapter 5.

SUMMARY:

- Emotions evolved as a mechanism to deal with emergency situations without conscious awareness.
- We can't interfere directly with emotional

reactions to a trigger.
- We can learn to recognize when a reaction starts.
- We are not able to completely prevent the first impulse triggered by an emotion.

During the refractory period:
- Attention is focused; that is useful for mobilizing resources.
- Information is filtered:
    - Only information that supports the emotion gets through, both from the environment/external events and from memory.
    - Information is distorted/misinterpreted to feed the emotion.

CHAPTER 3
THE SEVEN
UNIVERSAL EMOTIONS

As we have established, emotions have a crucial influence on our perception of the environment and operate automatically without our conscious interference.

However, could emotions be innate and universal, as Charles Darwin presumed? Is it probable that we all share universal triggers and experience their influence in the same way? Is it possible to recognize the emotions of strangers just by paying attention to their behavior?

In the mid-1900s, Paul Ekman, who was at the time just beginning his career, became convinced that nonverbal communication is socially learned and culturally conditioned. Nevertheless, a few lucky coincidences and a meeting with another behavioral psychologist, Silvan Tomkins, who intuited that emotions are innate, turned into the beginning of a series of fascinating discoveries.

After running experiments with emotion recognition and reactions on provocative video records, Ekman had to admit that his assumption seemed to be wrong. Tests with participants from Chile, Argentina, Brazil, Japan, and the United States showed somewhat similar data. That was an exciting outcome, since results that disprove an initial hypothesis usually appear to be more credible.

Still, that was not enough to reach a final conclusion. Another lucky coincidence was a tape of a motion picture film that Carleton Gajdusek took while studying slow viruses that were affecting a dying-out Stone Age tribe in Papua New Guinea called the Fore. Gajdusek was focused on studying the virus itself (he later received a Nobel Prize in medicine for research in this area), so he happily handed over the tapes for psychological research. Ekman and his colleague Friesen had spent six long months studying motion pictures, getting more and more convinced that they had found proof of the universality of emotions. Observing this relatively isolated and closed culture, they didn't register any expression that would appear alien or unfamiliar; what's more, they could recognize many familiar expressions and make judgments concerning emotional states and even predict intentions of the Fore people.

Inspired by these results, Ekman launched two expeditions (1967 and 1968) to New Guinea to study another isolated tribe of Fore people. Almost two years of studies allowed him to distinguish six universal emotions: anger, fear, surprise, sadness, disgust, and happiness. Later studies added contempt to the list.

Continuing their work, Ekman and Friesen wrote the first Atlas of the Face and developed a tool called the *facial action coding system* (FACS). FACS is used as a source of truth for most applications that focus on the automation of facial and emotion recognition, as well as computer graphics, cartoon animation, and humanization of robots.

While we are teaching machines to express and recognize emotions, have you ever asked yourself how good you actually are when it comes to it?

The latest research, including my own, allows us to conclude that females have an intuitive advantage in emotion recognition. Women, in fact, may be predisposed genetically when it comes to this skill. In the context of Darwin's theory of evolution, it makes total sense: Women, on average physiologically weaker and responsible for a progeny, had to be extra cautious about an environment, where correct evaluation of a situation could be crucial for survival.

Nevertheless, the ability to recognize emotions in yourself and others can be learned and significantly improved over a short period of time. This is going to be our next task. We will go through a detailed description of each of the seven universal emotions, analyzing their triggers and functions. By doing so, we will learn ways to recognize them by visual and audible cues and sensations.

Surprise

Surprise is the most rapid emotion that appears as a reaction to an unexpected event, and it lasts only for a second or two. Its purpose is to draw attention to something you have been exposed to unexpectedly, and to provide a quick estimation of its meaning. That is why genuine surprise so quickly fades out and switches to the next emotion that concludes the evaluation.

If you suddenly notice unknown shoes in the corridor as you enter your home, and the next moment the lights switch on, and all your friends are there wearing silly colorful hats and singing "Happy Birthday" to you, most likely your initial surprise will turn into happiness.

If you suddenly notice unknown shoes in the corridor as you are entering home, and the next moment you see a total stranger coming out of the room, your initial surprise will turn into fear. However, people with bad intentions are unlikely to take their shoes off, so it could be an old family friend or a forgotten uncle.

If you enter your home and suddenly step into a puddle that your puppy accidentally left there, your initial surprise may turn into disgust or anger.

As you can see in the illustration that follows, that's how you look like while experiencing surprise: the eyes widen, eyebrows raise, and the jaw drops. You pull back as if trying to create a space between you and the source of the surprise, increasing your observation area.

Besides being triggered by actual emotions, facial expressions can be emblematic. For example, if you want to show your friends how surprised you are by the party they have organized, you might hold your expression longer than a second and even repeat it a few times. While you are not surprised anymore, you will keep communicating the feeling, consciously or unconsciously, knowing that it's the expected reaction:

The Seven Universal Emotions

Surprise	
Universal trigger	Sudden, unexpected movement
Function	To focus attention
Posture	Head move or step away
Sensation	Attentive
Vocal signal	Momentary intake of breath

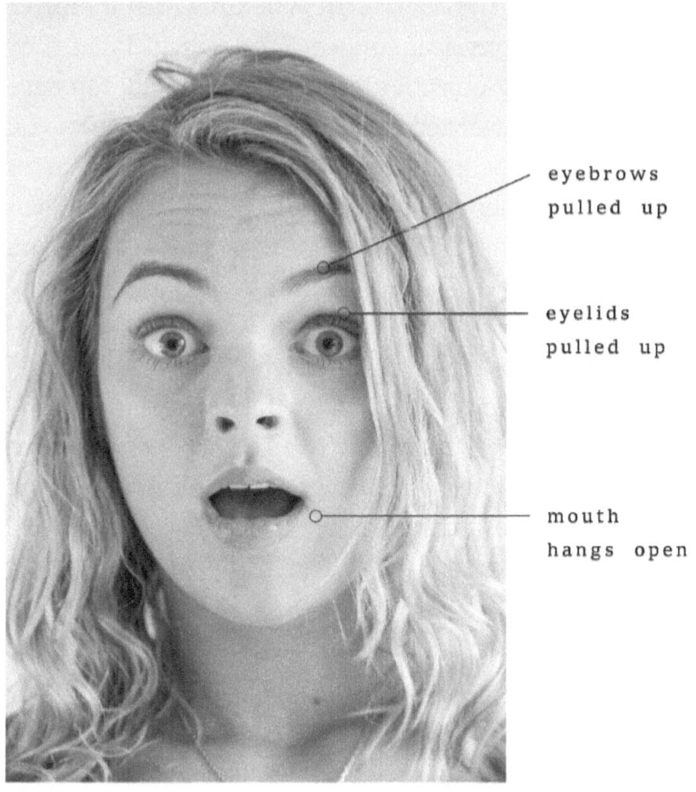

Fear

Surprise is usually recognized and understood by most of us, but it is very often confused with an expression of fear. Indeed, facial cues are quite similar for both emotions: wide eyes, raised eyebrows, parted mouth. But there are conceptual differences.

While surprise is a sign of an unexpected, novel event, fear responds to a threat of harm. The universal theme of fear is the loss of physical support (the fear of falling) or when a threatening object enters the visual field. I'm sure that you have experienced that sudden freezing when you notice movement behind your back out of the corner of your eye—the momentary panic of unknown danger. Then it turns out it was just a shadow or a neighbor's cat. So you breathe out with a smile, feeling silly and slightly embarrassed.

In our ancestors' time, though, when the environment was much less safe, the ability to be prepared for any situation played an essential role in survival. Fear prepares us to take care of our well-being: to freeze and become motionless to avoid a dangerous step and/or stay hidden from the potential source of danger, or to flee as quickly as possible.

If you have ever experienced a near-accident while driving a vehicle or while standing or walking on an unstable surface, your facial expression looked like the illustration that follows. When you experience fear, your eyebrows are not only raised but also brought together; your jaw tenses, and your mouth stretches horizontally. Your heart rate increases, and your hands turn cold as the blood is pushed toward your legs, enabling you to run away as fast as possible.

As soon as the dangerous moment has passed, your heart rate returns to normal, the feeling of coldness fades away, and the tension in your body drops.

The ability to recognize fear in others allows us to identify whether something unsafe is going on in our surroundings. If the source of fear is unknown, consciously or unconsciously, we instantly become more alert, while our brain begins to search for an explanation, usually finding it independently whether it matches the initial source or not. That phenomenon makes fear a highly contagious emotion:

Fear	
Universal trigger	Threat of harm
Function	Avoid or reduce harm
Posture	Freeze or move away
Sensation	Coldness, constriction
Vocal signal	Higher pitch

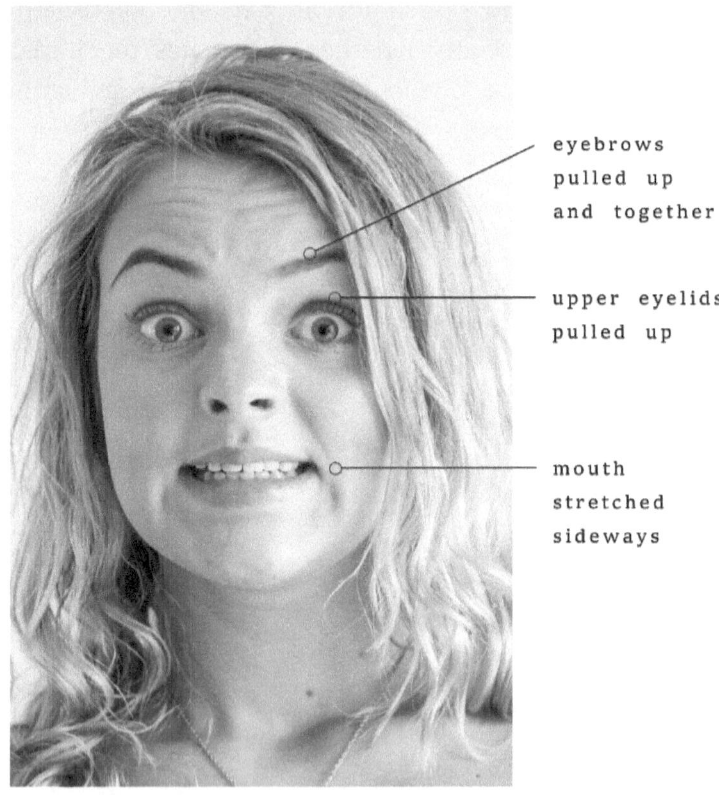

Anger

Have you ever asked yourself, why am I getting angry? You may think that every time, the reason is different: somebody made a nasty comment behind your back, the government made a bad decision, your boss was unfair, the airport queue is moving too slowly.

In reality, the cause is always the same—something or somebody appears as an obstacle between you and your goal. In the examples above: you want to keep your face and reputation, you want your country to be ruled by intelligent and altruistic people, you want to be appreciated for what you do at work, and finally you want to pass the airport queue to be in time for the flight or to enjoy a duty-free shop or a restaurant.

Anger is commonly perceived as a negative, unwanted emotion. At the same time, if used constructively, it allows us to persevere in the face of difficulty. It pushes us further and empowers us to fight for what we want to achieve.

How quickly one gets angry, and how far the expression of it goes, strongly depends on individual differences, temper, and even physiology. Nevertheless, you can always expect anger as a response to anger, because in most cases you are becoming an obstacle for your opponent.

Your angry face looks frightening: eyebrows pulled together and down, eyes narrowed with a glare, lips tensed and rolled in. Blood rushes toward the upper part of your body, preparing your arms for a fight and coloring your face red.

Anger modifies your appearance to demonstrate to others that nothing can stand between you and your goal.

This behavior can be seen even in very young infants if you put a toy almost within their reach, but as they try to get it, you withdraw it:

Anger	
Universal trigger	Interference with a goal
Function	Stop interference, eliminate threat to the goal
Posture	Head/chin forward, body puffed
Sensation	Heat, pressure cooker
Vocal signal	Edge, harsh, loud

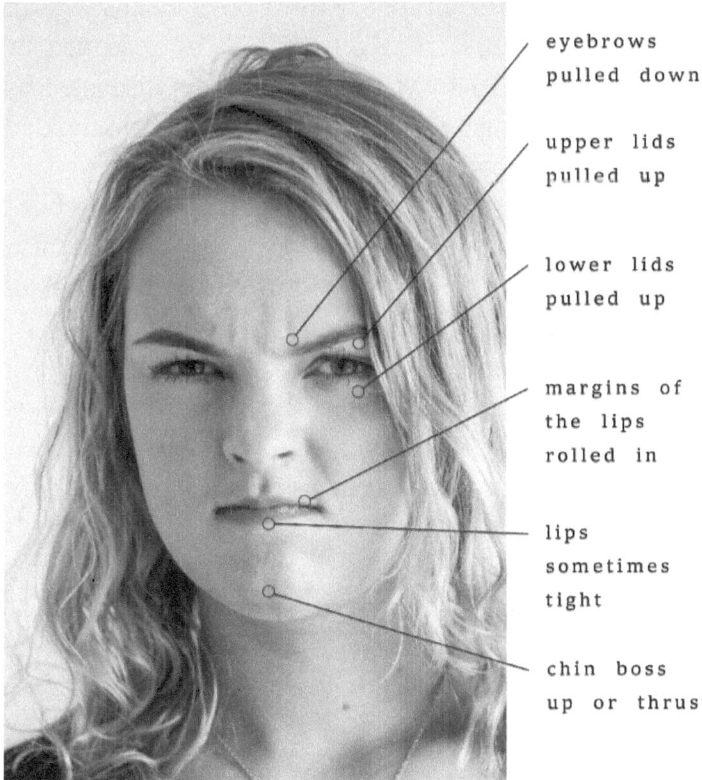

Disgust

Probably the easiest way to understand disgust is by doing the following: Take a glass of water and spit in it. Would you like to drink it now? If you belong to the majority of the population, you wouldn't. Even just imagining it makes you pull back, your nose wrinkled, and your upper lip rising up.

The most likely evolutionary function of disgust was to protect our ancestors from getting sick by poisoned or spoiled food. That is why we immediately get disgusted by numerous smells, such as rotten meat, tainted fish, molded French cheese, garbage bins, and vomit.

Another source of potential sickness would have been infections coming from ill animals or tribesmen. That also explains why most of us get disgusted at the sight of infected wounds, smelly breath, and ulcers.

But the wisdom of nature makes an exception: It suspends disgust toward people and creatures we love, allowing us to take care of them when in need. For example, mothers do not feel revulsion every time they are changing a diaper for their baby or cleaning their baby's vomit from their clothes.

Between lovers, disgust is also suspended, changing our perception of a partner's tongue and genitals. According to recent studies, our levels of disgust decline the more sexually aroused we are.

It's possible to say that further decline in disgust in intimacy signifies a strengthening of love. On the other hand, an increase in disgust in a close relationship often signifies distancing and troubles in paradise. Interestingly, research suggests that people have more trouble identifying micro-expressions of disgust in people they most care about, instead often perceiving it as anger:

Disgust	
Universal trigger	Something offensive
Function	Get away from
Posture	Turned away from, distant
Sensation	Revulsion, nausea
Vocal signal	"Yuck!"

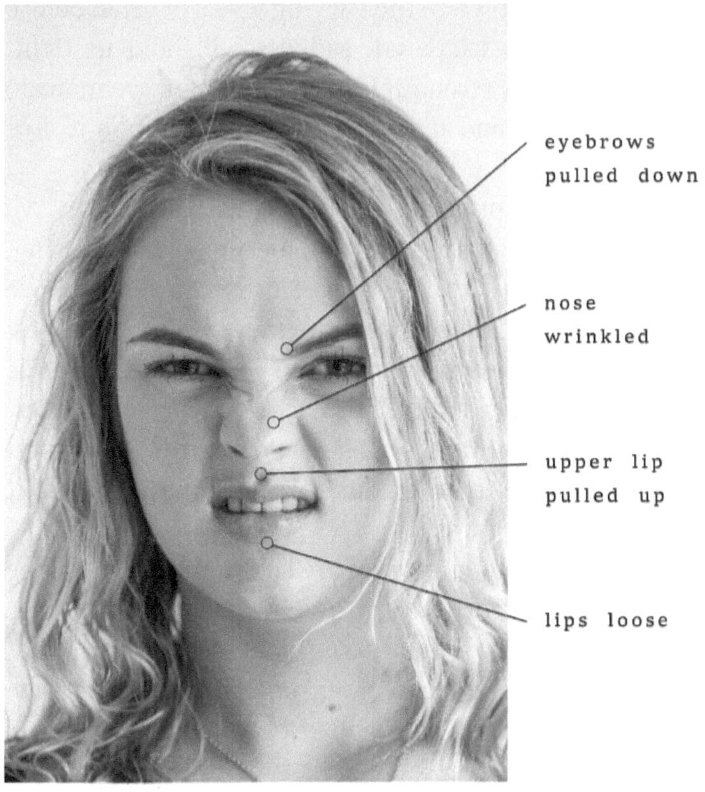

Sadness

The most powerful source of sadness is the loss of a loved one. Death, separation, and break-ups bring us to deepest, sometimes unbearable levels of this emotion.

For the other emotions we have discussed, the trigger is always temporary: We can avoid it or change it, like in the case of anger. But the major trigger for sadness is loss, which is often irreversible. That makes sadness a long-lasting emotion that may go up to the level of complete agony, then calm down to the varying levels of grief, before rising again. Once triggered, sadness will hold us tight, taking away all our strength until the moment we manage to accept the loss and figure out how to continue to live further.

Sadness often precedes or alternates with anger. We want to get back whatever or whomever we are missing, and if we identify someone as the cause of our loss, we direct rage at them. Sometimes, the cause is just ourselves: How stupid or inattentive can we be? Sometimes, it can be life itself, or a God that didn't protect us or our loved ones, or nature that is cruel and senseless. Sometimes, it is a rival in love who dared to enter our relationship and break it apart.

Luckily, not all of our losses are so dramatic. We can be sad about a lost opportunity, a stolen wallet, or sunglasses forgotten in a restaurant. In cases when we get back what we thought was gone forever, our emotion can transform instantly to happiness and relief.

The vital function of sadness is to issue a call for help. It is hard to cope with an irreversible trigger without the support of others, and nature provides us with this powerful tool—the emotion that will let others know how we feel and how much we need them now.

When we feel sad, our muscles lose tone. Shoulders drop. Eyelids get loose. Corners of the lips are pulled down. The inner corners of the eyebrows are raised. Our throat gets sore, eyes water. Everything about our appearance screams, "Come and hug me":

Sadness	
Universal trigger	Loss of a valued person, object, or opportunity
Function	Call for help
Posture	Loss of muscle tone, slack body
Sensation	Sore throat, aching and/or watery eyes
Vocal signal	Softer voice, sobbing

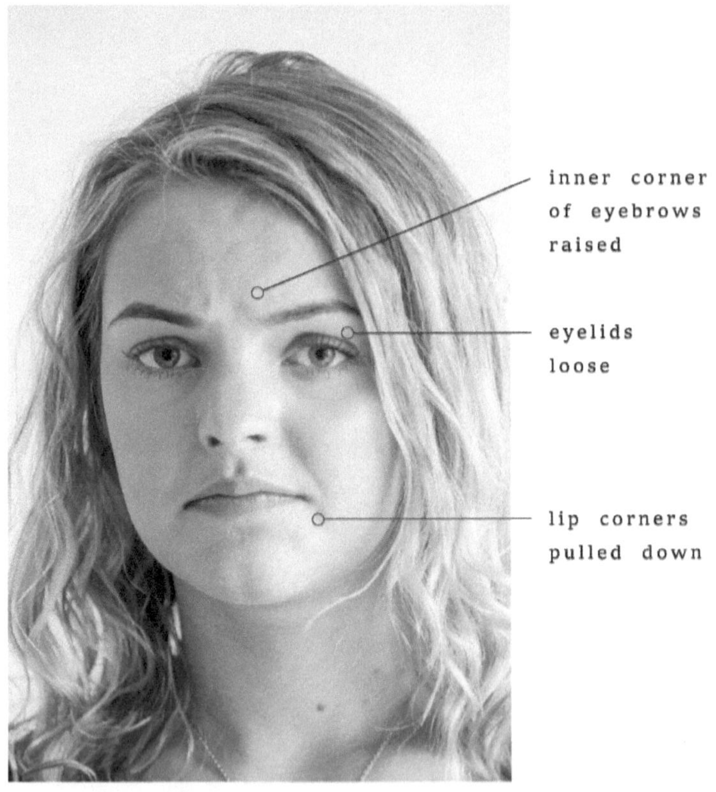

Contempt

It's easy to confuse the expression of contempt with a smile. But this asymmetric expression, when the lip corner is pulled up at one side only, has a totally different meaning. Unsurprisingly, it is often observed on photos and videos of celebrities, because it says "I'm better than you."

This emotion is only experienced concerning people or their actions. The feeling of being superior to someone triggers contempt. Moreover, contempt is often blended with another emotion, depending on what triggered it. If one sees or hears about an immoral action, you may think "I would never do that," and your contempt blends with anger or disgust. If a peer or competitor says or does something stupid, contempt can be blended with joy.

It is known that alpha male gorillas and chimpanzees show contempt toward young pretenders to their position in the community, which is often enough to ward off their attempts without any physical engagement.

That explains why women often find images of men with asymmetric smiles more attractive: It shows as confidence and superiority toward other males. Such a man can be perceived as the best pick for mating. Unfortunately, the owner of such an attitude is usually not the best for building a relationship with.

Contempt can often be observed during business meetings, where everyone assumes to know better than others. However, this emotion can also be directed toward oneself. One example: when we feel upset that a great idea didn't come to our mind first, but was instead expressed by a colleague. Or when we think of past events we are not proud of, or when we are unable to take a brave action and stand up for what we believe in.

When one experiences contempt for other people, it is often a pleasant feeling:

Contempt	
Universal trigger	Feeling of superiority
Function	Assert own superiority
Posture	Look "down your nose"
Sensation	Feels pleasant/good
Vocal signal	Smug sound

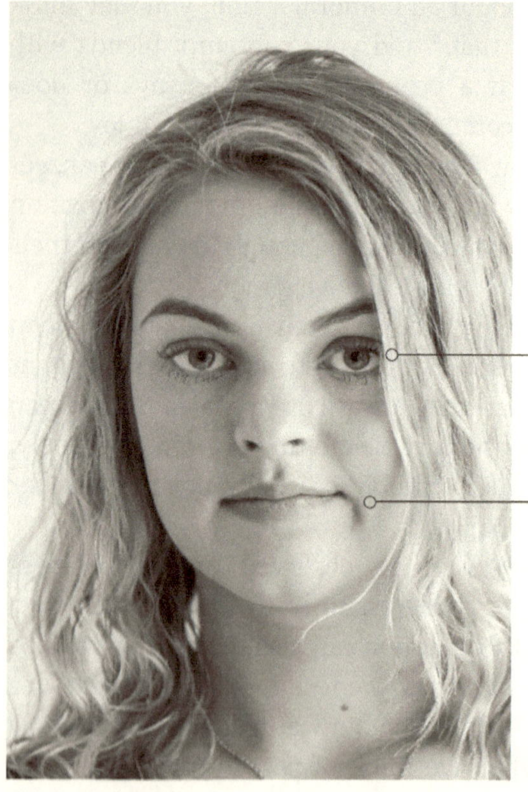

Happiness

Happiness is both the most intuitive and the most sophisticated emotion. The universal trigger for it is pleasure, but what brings us that pleasure can vary. Until recently, it was not very well understood.

Wrapping up in a warm, soft plaid and watching the cold evening outside through the window, chatting with best friends or family and drinking hot chocolate or mulled wine—that would definitely make me happy right now, and I'm smiling while writing these lines. Think about how many different sensations there are: touch, taste, smell; the feelings of comfort, coziness, and good company; the feeling of being accepted, understood. A smile communicates to others our friendliness, openness, and good intentions. It tells the world that we come in peace and mean no harm to anyone. Maybe that is why, in some countries and cultures, the smile became a part of social courtesy and lost its genuineness. We can try to fool each other, but it is more difficult to betray our nature. A genuine smile always differs from the social one.

There are many triggers for pleasure, but not all of them lead us to happiness. That is why a better name for this emotion would be joy. It is a moment when our brain identifies pleasure and sends forth the signal for a genuine smile. Some of these pleasures lead us toward well-being and harmony, but some of them make us overeat or turn us into shopaholics.

Happiness is a state we all are looking for. The moment when everything seems right, like a child being born, like sunshine after a thunderstorm, like a warm hand holding yours, ensuring that everything is going to be fine:

Happiness	
Universal trigger	Pleasure
Function	Social signal of friendliness
Posture	Elevated
Sensation	Warmth
Vocal signal	Exhale, laughter

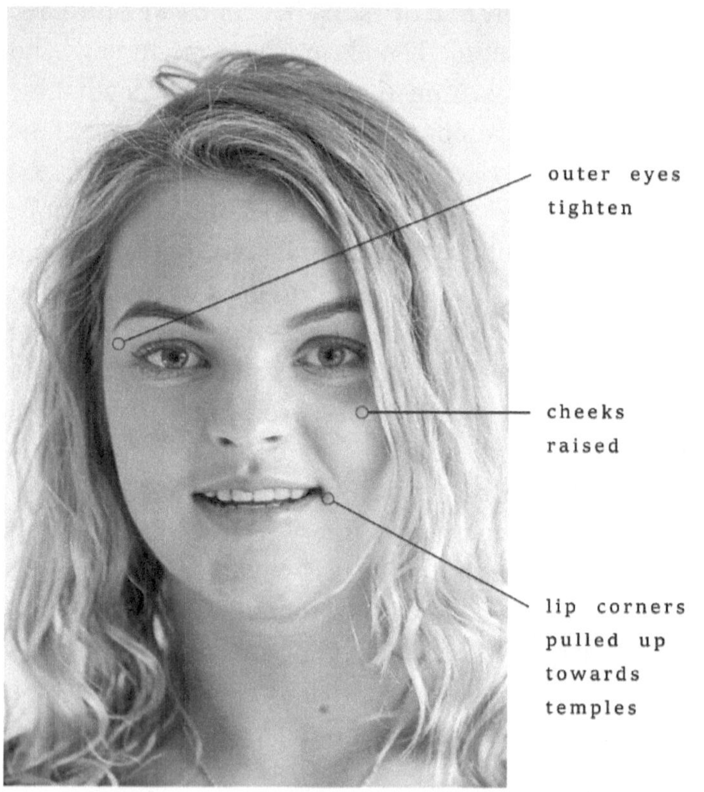

SUMMARY

It is important to mention that the illustrations in this chapter show classic facial expressions that can be observed when the intensity of the emotion is medium or high. If a person applies self-restrictions or display rules (see Chapter 5), specific facial muscles can be controlled and the emotion appears less prominently on the face. Moreover, in real life, we often experience a mix of emotions, and that will be reflected by our facial expressions, which represent a blend of cues. Nevertheless, micro-expressions always flash across our face before we are able to restrict them, giving away our emotional impulses. Going further, Paul Ekman developed a framework for recognizing lies based on micro-expressions and other nonverbal behavior. The method is based on an ability to identify desynchronization in five communication channels and further exploration of possible reasons for that. For example, if you declare that you are happy to hear a certain piece of news, but your facial expressions show no corresponding sign of the emotion, that would be marked by an observer as a discrepancy.

To practice what you have learned in this chapter, try the following exercises:

• Recall a moment when you experienced one of the emotions (always choose memories with emotional intensity just a little bit higher than average). Try to remember being in that moment and observe changes within your body and facial expressions.

• Take a mirror and try to replicate the facial

expressions presented in the illustrations. When you think your expression is correct, try to hold it for a while and observe changes in your body and sensations. Always finish this exercise with a smile.

• Try to pay attention to the facial expressions of people in your surroundings. Look at them nonjudgmentally, without making any conclusions about the reasons for their emotional states.

CHAPTER 4
DISPLAY RULES

If emotions are universal, why do people express them differently? The answer is straightforward: we all apply norms that are dictated to us by family and society. From childhood on, we learn and adopt acceptable emotional behaviors, adjusting our expressiveness accordingly.

I once witnessed the following scene. My neighbor was having a conversation with her five-year-old son. The boy was furious about something and kept repeating, "I'm angry! Oh, I'm so angry!" My neighbor, a very calm lady, kept replying to him, "Don't be angry." The boy continued protesting: "Why can't I be angry if I feel like it?" His mom answered, "Because it's not nice."

That is precisely how we learn to suppress and hide our emotions, instead of analyzing them and trying to understand what causes them and how to deal with it. We learn to look "nice" to not be judged.

Every family has a different level of acceptance regarding emotional expressiveness toward family members, depending on gender, age, role, culture, and familial history. The way people express themselves with siblings differs from the way they act toward a mother, father, grandparents, and so on. People who grew up in an emotionally challenging environment, with firm authority and rules that limit displays of emotion, may struggle to express their emotions freely further in life, while becoming very keen at recognizing them in others.

We learn to hide some of our genuine emotions to be socially accepted and/or not to be punished for it. At the same time, we learn to expose emblematic emotions when expected and rewarded by others. In Western cultures, one of the most common things kids learn is how to adapt to failure. I'm sure you remember from childhood or have observed at least once while playing board games or competitive sports: If you lose, children can go into a deep sadness and start crying. Another possible reaction is to become angry and begin fighting the perceived obstacle that prevented you from winning. Usually, this obstacle is the winner and the other players.

There can be a wide variety of feedback to these behaviors. Other kids may laugh and tease the loser or refuse to play again. Parents or other adults may frighten the child to be excluded from the playing group in the future. In a majority of cases, social feedback in such situations is negative. That is how we learn to take our failures with a poker face.

During childhood, we also learn to modulate our emotional expressiveness in the presence of strangers and people of different authority levels. For example, in many cultures, parents will hush a child who is behaving expressively in public, whether the child is laughing too loudly, crying, screaming in anger or fear, or spitting out their food in disgust. That is how we learn which attitudes are tolerated in a private environment and which have to be muffled or hidden in public. Indeed, recent research confirms that display rules vary by context. People show less emotional expressiveness at work for all universal emotions. And employees in Eastern cultures show less expressiveness for anger, sadness, and fear compared to employees in the United States.

More differences can be observed on a national scale: Cultures that have developed in warmer climates are usually more expressive and have fewer gender-related limitations compared to cold-weather cultures.

Religion is another important influence. In many cases, religion dictates what should we feel in various circumstances and how we are allowed to express it without risk of committing a sin. For example, in Orthodox Christianity, loud, open-mouthed laughter is considered wicked. It is strongly suggested to express joy with a smile that doesn't show teeth. That is why it is quite unlikely for you to ever see Orthodox priests or nuns laughing out loud in public. As we know, other branches of Christianity do not necessarily share this rule, though most religions have rules governing emotional displays in places of religious importance: churches, temples, mosques, and shrines.

In general, every culture has its own rules governing emotional displays that are acceptable during important social events like weddings and funerals. In some countries, funerals are sad, silent events filled with tears, which cannot be interrupted by smiles or any sign of joy. In other countries, for example Ghana, funerals are accompanied with cheerful music, dancing, and bright, colorful coffins.

In some cultures, it would be odd if, during a wedding, the bride and groom did not express their joy. It would raise suspicion that the couple is not exercising free will in declaring their union. In other cultures, a bride has to emanate sadness and even cry a few days or weeks in advance to ensure the proper appearance at this important life event. Any expression of joy, in this case, would be unacceptable.

In many cultures, boys are conditioned to suppress fear and sadness, because society dictates that men should always appear brave and strong. There is a wrongheaded association between sadness and weakness. The idea that "boys don't cry" takes away a young male's ability to call for help. As a consequence, the ability to empathize may not fully develop. The belief that "boys can't be afraid," meanwhile, robs them of their ability to evaluate risk properly.

The era of social media introduces new display rules and a new level of threat to our emotional well-being. People interact less and less in actual reality and often expose themselves to an extended group of total strangers who gain access to their lives and feelings.

Next time you post anything publicly on social media, think about how you expose yourself with your thoughts, your joy, your sadness, your anger, and your fear to total strangers who don't know you, or who only know you superficially. They don't know your life, and any feedback they leave has little to do with you. Most of them are solving their own problems and reflecting moods that have nothing to do with what you shared. You might think, "But of course, who wouldn't know that?" This is exactly where danger hides: We become shallower and faker in a social media environment in order to maintain appearances that mask reality and do not lead to harm from strangers. Since a big part of our daily communication occurs on social media, this shallowness and fakeness seeps into our lives without us noticing it.

So what is the nature of display rules? Are they helpful or harmful? That strongly depends on the way we deal with them. Display rules can help us to communicate efficiently. They prevent us from overreacting and help us handle our social image. Learning about display rules of people you interact with, especially if they belong to a different culture, can be the key to successful communication. At the same time, if we are unaware of our own display rules, they might hold us back from emotional expressiveness in situations when it is required and expected. If we continuously suppress emotions according to display rules without further proper elaboration, it can lead to disorders and uncontrolled emotional explosions. For example, one may hide and suppress anger caused by a situation at work, and then release it in ugly fashion on family members at home.

I often hear around how people tell each other "Don't be angry," "Don't be sad," "Don't be afraid." We tend to impose our expectations without helping each other to deal with our emotions. I wish we could handle the emotional expressiveness of one other with genuine interest and support, helping each other to figure out the reasons and functions of those emotions, and directing them to a more constructive path.

SUMMARY

Display rules are learned throughout an entire life under contextual and environmental influences. They define our emotional expressiveness in various situations.

Awareness of our own display rules and the display rules of others can improve communication and emotional health.

Try to analyze what display rules are shared within

your country, your immediate surroundings, your community, and your family. Ask yourself the following questions:

- Are they useful or harmful?
- What display rules have you noticed in other people?
- Have you ever been in a situation where you unconsciously broke display rules?
- How did you deal with that situation?

CHAPTER 5
REGRETTABLE QUARRELS

51

We get into quarrels, heated discussions, and fights when we are angry. As we've discussed, constructive anger gives us energy and allows us to work through obstacles in pursuit of our goals. But what makes angry episodes regrettable?

Think about your last episode and write down any reasons you regret it.

We will discuss the root causes of regrettable angry behavior based on examples from real life.

Wrongly Identified Obstacles

Imagine a boy who is very passionate about soccer. He trains every day and dreams of becoming a professional player and winning a World Cup for his country. A girl, who is his classmate, constantly teases him by saying, "You will never be that good" or "You will never play on a national team." That drives the boy crazy. He argues with her, shouts, leaves the classroom in a rage and, at one point, even hits her. From the perspective of the teacher and classmates, this reaction is unreasonable and disproportionate to the girl's behavior, especially if she does it on the sly. Finally, all the attention goes to the behavior of the victim and the boy's suffering doubles, because he doesn't get support from those around him.

What is going wrong here?

The girl most likely is trying to attract attention. Considering that the boy's thoughts are completely occupied with soccer, she picks up the only topic that he responds to. Another explanation could be that she is solving some internal problem of her own, like envy or fear of failure, if her dreams are likewise lofty. However, she is not the main target of our consideration. What I would like to bring to your attention is the question of why the boy overreacts so strongly.

As we have established, we get angry when we see an obstacle to our goals. In the situation described above, the boy wrongly identifies the teasing girl as an obstacle, a barrier on the way to his dream of becoming a great player. Indeed, she uses words and phrases that can trigger this impression. However, looking at the situation objectively, it becomes obvious that the girl has zero influence on the boy's future career. She is not competition; she doesn't influence any important decisions or selection processes.

That mistake of identification causes the anger that looks unjustified from the outside. That in turn causes a lot of problems for the boy at school and at home, because he comes back in a bad mood and teachers reach out to his parents with complaints.

What would be the usual scenario of dealing with this

situation? The boy would be told to suppress his anger and ignore the girl. That would naturally lead to bigger explosions in the future, because the girl would feel empowered to push harder, and the boy would accumulate his anger until the moment he can no longer hold it in. A more effective strategy would be to go with him through his anger path and let him figure out that the obstacle that triggers his anger exists only in his imagination. This realization automatically reduces the levels of his reaction.

Unreasonable Goals

Now let's consider another case with a classic situation: a teenager is planning to attend a late-night party or go on a trip with friends. For one reason or another, this teenager's parents refuse to support the idea and forbid it. Everyone knows what happens next: insisting, arguing, shouting, crying. After some time, usually when the goal is not relevant anymore, this behavior is recognized as regrettable.

Similar situations can happen between family members, colleagues, and friends when a goal requires commitment or support from others, but they are not able or not willing to provide it for one reason or another. When making decisions, plans, and building up expectations, we often forget to analyze upfront what is required for others to go along with us.

To use the earlier example: When teenagers make plans for a late outing, getting a tattoo, or attending a music festival, they often forget to ask themselves how safe it looks for their parents and how the required financial support fits their budget.

When we ask colleagues to perform extra work or delegate tasks to them that are not an official part of their role, we often forget to consider why it would seem like a good idea to them. What other plans and commitments might they already have? When we ask a friend to help cover up our affair or support us in a fight, we forget to consider that it might go against their values. When we ask family members to stay with our kids or bring grandma to the hospital, we forget to ask ourselves how convenient and manageable it is for them.

Obviously, when people refuse to behave according to our plans, we perceive them as an obstacle.

False Script Initiation

In Chapter 3, I mentioned triggers that can initiate emotional scripts in inadequate situations. I've told the story of my own script that can be tipped off by the simple question, "Did you take the scissors?"—or any other object, for that matter.

Let's discuss a few more examples. Imagine a girl who, during her childhood, had a tendency to be slightly overweight. Her family tried to control her eating habits by putting restrictions on desserts, sweet drinks, and portion sizes. On top of that, some family members teased her, making jokes about her body. The girl, who always loved food, developed the script that connects any comments regarding her body shape with these restrictions. Imagine now that she grew up into a sporty woman with a model's body. Any comments regarding her shape, even positive ones, would still trigger an immediate spark of anger, especially coming from a family member.

Now let's come back to the boy from our first example. Because his dream of becoming a soccer player was mocked by the mischievous girl for an extended period of time, sparking a strong emotional outcome, he could develop a script that triggers every time someone, especially a woman, questions or doubts his plans. As questioning a partner's plans is common in a close relationship, such a script potentially can be quite harmful. In the future, a simple question such as, "Are you sure it's a good idea?" or "Are you confident that you could do it?" coming from a girlfriend, wife, or a colleague could trigger the old script with high anger levels.

Emotional scripts are one reason why it can be so hard to overcome old, undesirable patterns in relationships. Even if situations and intentions change, our brain still tries to adjust to a story we already know and have gotten used to, even if it is toxic.

Refractory Period and Amygdala Hijack

Finally, let's discuss a reason that anger grows and does not let us calm down, looking at the example of quarrels that rise out of "nothing." Imagine a husband has a few hours of commuting time to his place of work. Naturally, it is a tiring process that can be interrupted by traffic jams and other annoying obstacles. On the way back home, he is in an irritable mood. Meanwhile, his wife needs to plan dinner and decide if the kids should be waiting for his arrival or not. Therefore, she calls him with a question: "When do you expect to be home?" This question lands on his irritable mood and his guilty feelings for being late often, so he takes her question as an accusation and replies, with anger in his tone, "I have no idea."

Obviously, such an answer cannot satisfy the wife, who needs to decide how to proceed with dinner. So she repeats her question again, asking, "Shall we wait for you or not?" With this second question, anger appears also in her voice, because he doesn't provide her the necessary information and becomes an obstacle for her planning. Moreover, she does not appreciate his tone, which she assumes is directed toward her.

Her second question confirms the husband's (incorrect) assumption that she is accusing him of being late. He starts a verbal attack/defense. As his attitude becomes a more evident and unavoidable obstacle to her peaceful evening, she gets angry as well. Now they are both in a refractory period, during which all information they receive from each other is interpreted in a way that feeds their anger.

As anger grows in intensity, a phenomenon called the *amygdala hijack* can occur. The amygdala is the part of the brain that governs emotional behavior and motivation. When levels of anger or fear requiring a fight-or-flight response cross a certain threshold, the amygdala takes full control of our perception and behavior. From that moment on, it blocks access to the neocortex and the capacity for rational thinking. This "emotional brain" processes information much faster, but often with a twist. Because of that, attempts by both quarrelling sides to get back to a peaceful state can be misinterpreted and refused. Usually, these sorts of fights can end only by breaking the contact (hanging up the phone, leaving the room, going for a walk) and distracting yourself from what just happened. Often, as soon as the amygdala calms down, it is hard to explain why you got so angry, because rationally there was no justifiable reason.

SUMMARY

The main factor that makes angry episodes regrettable is a reaction that is disproportionate to the trigger. Angry episodes can ruin reputations and valuable relationships. That is why it is important to stay aware of one's own triggers and attitude patterns and try to analyze the causes.

Anger that we can observe in others signals to us that something is going wrong. In those situations, it is worth stepping back for a moment and trying to analyze what is happening with the other person, before your own amygdala gets activated and shuts down your rational thinking.

Moreover, if you stay attentive to your own state, it is possible to recognize that your emotions have already been triggered. In this case, the best possible strategy is to walk away from the heated conversation. You should inform the other party that you recognize their feelings concerning the subject, but need time to calm down so that you can proceed with the discussion later, if it will be still relevant. Walking away from a quarrel, make sure that you do not relitigate it in your memories, keeping the dialogue active in your head. Distract yourself fully with an activity unrelated to the topic of the argument.

Think about your angry episodes and try to answer the questions:

- What is your hottest trigger and why?
- What was a cause of your regrettable anger episodes?

- Wrongly identified obstacle
- Unreasonable goal
- False script initiation
- Refractory period and amygdala hijack

CHAPTER 6
GUILT VERSUS SHAME

Every now and then, we all do things that are judged by society as wrong or impermissible.

Sometimes it happens by accident; for instance, when a child drops food on their new clothing, or when you break your mother-in-law's favorite vase with a clumsy move, or by mistake reveal somebody's secret.

Sometimes it happens because we act selfishly and do not consider the impact of our actions on others; for example, when we are too excited or busy with life events, we might forget to call our parents, congratulate friends on a birthday, or ignore somebody's call for help.

And sometimes we do something perfectly aware that it won't be accepted well. Knowing that it breaks commitments or laws, the desire to get what we want is way too strong, and we hope not to get caught. Cheating on exams, having a love affair while in a relationship, not paying bills or taxes, and stealing are all apt examples.

No matter which of the three cases we are dealing with, it is always difficult to admit our fault before others. Every time it feels unpleasant, and most of us try to avoid such an exposure and confession at any cost.

Why does that happen? Supposedly, it has deep anthropological roots. To be a part of the community was an essential condition of survival for our ancestors; being excluded from the community would be a severe threat, leading to suffering or even death. Thus, the possibility of exclusion from the community developed as one of our strongest basic fears. This exclusion usually happens by the principle "you don't fit us," meaning you don't share the same values, don't have the required qualities, and you are harmful to the community. That is exactly what "shame on you" represents. It addresses personal qualities that led to an unacceptable action. According to research, we can experience shame as early as 15 months as an innate feeling of being worthless and defective. Indeed, already from early childhood, we hear that "good boys don't do that" or "good girls would never do it." In those circumstances, to admit fault or a mistake is tantamount to acknowledging that you are not a good member worthy of the community. That is why shaming always leads to concealing.

Shame also causes us to generate numerous excuses in attempts to explain and justify our behavior. From that perspective, shame is not a constructive emotion. To an extent, it restrains us from changing our faulty behavior, because to change it means to admit that it was wrong. Hence, shame can even lead to self-exclusion from one group and a search for another where people are "as bad as me." That phenomenon can be observed among teenagers, who are especially vulnerable to it. Another example is in a criminal environment, where people who get into it even with a minor crime rarely recover socially and often sink deeper and deeper as they would always feel "worse than others" among people without criminal records.

We can conclude that shame and shaming don't have any positive outcome for anyone. They don't help a person to improve, and instead lead to lies, excuses, and distance.

In its turn, guilt is directed toward the action and its

outcome. While shame states, "You are a mistake," guilt says, "You made a mistake." It points to the action that one should repair and not repeat to avoid an undesirable impact on one's environment. The ability to experience guilt develops between ages 3 and 6, approximately at the same time as we learn to see the perspectives of other people and develop an ability to understand how they are affected by our actions.

Nevertheless, it is possible to define healthy and unhealthy guilt.

Healthy guilt is caused by the realization that our behavior can lead to harming the well-being of others and/or break objective definitions of right and wrong. The upshot is that recognition of such has a positive influence on one's personal growth, since it resolves as we repair the damage we caused.

Unlike in a case with shame, even admitting guilt gives a person relief, as it creates a distance between the person and the action, which has already happened and now belongs to the past.

From the other side, unhealthy guilt is caused by actions and behaviors that break unrealistically high standards or expectations. Unhealthy guilt is usually rooted in unrealistically high demands imposed by adults or authority figures, or developed by the need to please adults during early childhood. Unhealthy guilt leads to self-punishment instead of behavioral change and remains until we correct irrational beliefs about acceptable norms of behavior.

That is why both shaming and unhealthy guilt are often used by manipulators and family abusers. They create in the victim a constant feeling of unworthiness and defect, while instilling a belief that the abuser is the only company they can ever get. At the same time, stimulating unhealthy guilt, they push the victim to look for punishment and take it for granted.

According to Paul Ekman's research, both shame and guilt belong to the sadness family and have corresponding visual and vocal cues. Indeed, as we covered in Chapter 5, the main theme of sadness is loss, and in the case of shame and guilt, we experience a loss of face in front of others and a loss of trust.

Since the feeling of healthy guilt is strongly entangled with an ability to empathize, people with psychological disorders that negatively influence this ability are also hardly ever able to experience guilt, no matter how harmful their actions may be for others.

Nevertheless, if you want a person to confess or admit what they have done—and hopefully fix any damage, cooperate, and improve—you should avoid phrases that appeal to shame, and instead focus on communication that appeals to the feeling of guilt.

Try to pay attention to what you feel when you make a mistake and your way of dealing with it, as well as the manner in which people in your environment deal with it. It's important to remember that only healthy guilt leads to responsible approach, personal growth, and improvements in relationships.

Shame	Guilt
My son would never do this. Who even are you?	It was wrong to do it. I hope you'll never repeat it again.
Only bad people do it.	This action was unacceptable.
What kind of monster would do this?	What happened was really hurtful.
Shame Manipulation	Guilt Manipulation
Only the most degenerate, morally depraved, cretinous imbecile could fail to see the truth of my argument.	I don't care that you were busy with other tasks I've requested! I was counting on you to do this on time, as well, and you just ignored it! What should I do now?

SUMMARY

Shame and guilt are emotions from the sadness family, as the main theme is a loss of face, trust, respect, and love from others. Thus, they are often followed by corresponding visual and vocal cues.

However, besides being triggered by similar causes, they have opposite effects:

• Shame addresses personal qualities and triggers rejection and concealment.
• Guilt addresses the effect of the action and triggers confession, efforts to repair any damage, and self-improvement.

CHAPTER 7
FEARS AND PHOBIAS

As we discussed in Chapter 4, the theme of fear is a threat to our life.

Genetics explain why one of the most common phobias is the fear of heights, which translates into a fear of falling, and the fear of inconspicuous sources of danger, like snakes and spiders. Recognizing these sorts of threats was essential for our ancestors' survival.

We also develop many fears during childhood out of warnings adults give us. Parents and grandparents want to protect children from dangerous situations and sometimes go too far in that effort. That is how phobias of darkness, going outside alone, electricity, open windows, and many others can develop.

Older siblings and friends can give us unreasonable fears of imaginary evil by telling us spooky stories. The first fairy tales were told to scare children and prevent them from doing potentially dangerous things. Nowadays, mass media and the movie industry supply us with a variety of fears attuned to modern times. The fear of losing our job is a threat to our well-being and position in society. The fear of being not pretty, of being not good enough, of being abandoned, of being bullied, and of judgment are potential threats of exclusion from society. There are many more. Our lives are full of fears.

A phobia can develop from a particularly traumatic, life-threatening experience, as well. For example, nearly drowning can lead to an extreme fear of water.

When multiple fear-driving reasons combine, one needs strong self-efficacy and self-control to avoid falling into a phobia trap.

For example, my grandma used to tell me that if I touched frogs, my hands would get covered with warts. It was already a terrifying image by itself. Then one day, my classmate decided that throwing a frog down my shirt would be great fun. As you can imagine, for observers it definitely was. But not for me, as I was jumping, screaming, and imagining how my body would be covered with warts while cold, wet frog legs touched my skin. It took many years and much mental effort to mitigate this phobia.

So what distinguishes fear from phobia? Fear aims to protect us from danger and give us a moment to evaluate all the pros and cons of our next step, if it looks risky. Phobia, on the other hand, deals with unreasonable measures of imaginary danger and inflated ideas of risk. Phobia applies serious limitations and constraints on our way of living. For example, aerophobia, or fear of flying, limits the way one can travel.

The fear of getting a bad mark at school will push one to study harder, but a phobia of getting a bad mark will paralyze the mind and block the ability to perform up to one's capabilities.

Any phobia introduces a weak point to our existence, which can be exploited to manipulate our decisions and actions. Additionally, since emotions are contagious, there is always a possibility that we transmit our phobias to people we are close to: partners, relatives, kids. That is why working toward treating or overcoming a phobia is highly beneficial, to yourself and loved ones.

Depending on the degree of the phobia, it can be useful to look for professional help. In general, phobias can be treated by psychotherapy. One of the most popular techniques is exposure therapy, where the patient gradually moves forward to face the source of the specific phobia and related thoughts, feelings, and sensations. That helps to manage the emotions and reduce the anxiety.

Another way of dealing with a phobia is cognitive behavioral therapy, which involves exposure combined with techniques that help to change beliefs about the specific fear.

Sometimes therapy can be supported by medication that helps to reduce anxiety.

As an opposite phenomenon, people with amygdala dysfunction have problems experiencing fear, which can lead them into life-threatening situations without conscious realization of it.

Although I defined fear as an effective mechanism for potential risk evaluation, and phobia as a limiting mechanism based on unreasonable measures of risk, there is one topic that is difficult to classify: fear of the unknown. When we can clearly identify things, it gives us the comfort of awareness and the ability to predict how events will develop. This type of comfort is entirely independent of how happy or satisfied we feel about the current state of affairs.

Sometimes people complain about being unhappy at work or in a relationship, about the government, their friends' attitude toward them, colleagues, or family members, but at the same time they do absolutely nothing to change the situation.

That is why that type of comfort—the comfort of known

misery—is one of the most insidious things in our lives. It's a trap that holds us from taking a step from habitual toward better. People are ready to fight for their uncomfortable comfort zones because fear of the unknown transforms into fear of change. It can get us stuck in situations, preventing us from moving forward, away from unpleasant situations and bad relationships.

We fear change because we can't anticipate the outcome. Thoughts like "I don't know what will happen to me if..." and "I'm afraid it may get worse..." hold us back from action.

So what is a strategy to deal with this type of fear? Actually, very much the same as dealing with any other emotion: Start by rationalizing it. Instead of telling yourself a story of potential failures, begin asking yourself questions and searching for answers.

For example, let's say you are unhappy with a job you are doing. If you quit right now, you may lose a source of income, reducing your quality of life. However, you might have savings that would be enough for a certain period, or family members ready to support your decision. If that is not the case, what is the worst that can happen if you start looking for another job right now? You might not find it or get it. But then, in the very worst case, your situation just will not change. That would be an easy call, if not for a fear of failure and social judgment. "What will people think of me if I fail?" That you can figure out as well, by talking to people whose opinions you value. Maybe, instead of being judgmental of failure, they would be proud of your attempt. Maybe, if they care for your well-being and know your feelings and hopes, they would be motivated to provide support. Again, it would be an easy call, but what if you were to change jobs, only to realize the new one is even worse than the old one? To prevent this, you need to thoughtfully define in advance the criteria that are important for you, and make sure to verify them before making a final decision.

You'll never be sure unless you start exploring, reducing step-by-step the area of the unknown, lighting up the path in front of you.

SUMMARY

Like any other emotion, fear is a substantial part of our life. It helps us to identify potential danger, focus our awareness, and run life-saving scripts automatically. However, it is up to our rational thinking to verify and minimize risks related to the fears that prevent us from developing and moving on.

Try to answer the following questions:

• What role does fear play in your life?
• When is it helpful and when is it counterproductive?
• Does fear introduce limitations? Does it drive your choices?
• What is your usual strategy for dealing with fear?
• How could it be improved?

CHAPTER 8
SADNESS: THE CALL FOR HELP

Sadness is accompanied by a heaviness in the chest; it takes away our strength, and colors the world grey. It is probably the hardest emotion to handle. As we discussed in Chapter 4, the universal trigger for sadness is a loss of something or somebody important, valuable, and/or loved. Often it is irreversible, and that makes this emotion long lasting.

According to the Kübler-Ross model, there are five stages of grief we go through on the path to full recovery.

Denial: We don't want and refuse to believe what is happening and search for the ways to disprove it.

Anger: When we cannot find a way to disprove what is happening, we have to face the fact that our goal cannot be achieved. Anything we perceive as an obstacle to that goal becomes a target of our anger: our own stupidity, other people involved, God, destiny, and so on.

Bargaining: Here we try to solve the cause of our sadness or grief by negotiating with whomever we identify as problem solvers: people, the universe, God, and the like.

Depression: It is essential to not confuse this term with a clinical state, as this stage does not necessarily represent it. During this stage, we recognize our emotional state and need time to process it. It often leads to a temporary period of silence and isolation.

Acceptance: This stage comes with the realization that

there is nothing we can do to reverse the situation and life goes on despite what happened. This stage brings calmness and stabilizes our emotions.

Initially, Elisabeth Kübler-Ross developed this model reflecting on how people cope with loss of health and life. Later on, together with David Kessler, she extrapolated the model for various types of losses, such as loss of a job, opportunity, relationship, and so on. We do not always go through the stages sequentially, and even less often linearly. Some stages can pass so quickly that they may be unnoticeable, although it is useful for self-reflection to be aware of them.

Let's consider an example that happened to me a few years ago. During the holidays, I left my favorite sunglasses on a table in a hotel lobby. I realized only about thirty minutes later that they were missing. My first reaction was to look for them everywhere: my bag, pockets, drawers, bathroom, refusing to believe they could be gone (denial stage). Then I remembered that I took them with me to the lobby. I went there, searched again, and asked the hotel personnel. When that didn't bring any luck, I got irate: first at my own absence of mind, then at the situation, then at a hypothetical someone who might have taken the glasses (anger stage). Then for a short time, I sent prayers to who knows where, promising to be nice and always help others to find what they have lost (bargaining stage). After that, I sat for a few minutes in silence, very upset, processing the information that all my efforts were useless and my favorite sunglasses were gone forever (depression stage). Soon, I realized that they're just sunglasses; I shouldn't spoil my holidays being disturbed by this loss, and I needed to move on (acceptance stage).

In this example, it took me about half an hour to go through all the stages. Depending on the nature of the loss, it could take more or less time; some stages could return, and some pass very quickly.

Nevertheless, at every stage of grief, we need support. We need somebody to catch us when we are falling through it and hold us, whispering that we are not alone and that we are understood. Nature gave us sadness as a tool to signal our request for help and support.

Unfortunately, in many societies, sadness is often associated with weakness. From our childhood we start to hear from adults that something "is not worth crying over," or to "stop it already, this is not a big deal," or "c'mon girl, if you can't handle this, how will you handle real difficulty?" or "big boys don't cry," and so on.

That phenomenon can be explained by the latest research, which shows that we naturally feel less empathy and compassion for people who go through experiences we already went through in the past. Thus, as you can imagine, all the lost toys, bad marks at school, quarrels with friends, and teenage dramas that are experienced very intensely in the moment may look like minor issues for adults who went through these things and worse. Moreover, while in emotional distress we have a tendency to look for moral support among those who went through similar experiences and "have been in our shoes," but they are actually less likely to show compassion.

That is how we begin learning to hide our sadness. To suppress it. Because sharing it might seem useless, even unsafe, for our reputation.

But that's not exactly how nature designed it. Nature

made sadness the most contagious emotion to ensure that we get support from our environment. It provided us with mirror neurons to ensure our capability to empathize and feel what another person is feeling. It equips not only humans but animals with compassion and the ability to sacrifice their own interests to help others. When we emerge from a period of sadness supported by others, it helps create bonds and strengthen relationships.

There is a significant difference between showing sympathy and showing empathy. With sympathy, we recognize someone's state and wish them better. But we do not get emotionally involved or try to "feel" what they are going through. When we hear or say "Oh come on, get over it, it's not the end of the world," that is sympathy speaking.

Psychology defines three types of empathy:

• *Cognitive empathy* allows for an accurate analysis of the emotional state of another. It is the ability to take a perspective and see the situation in the same way they do.

• *Emotional empathy* allows others to feel what others are feeling. If that ability is not combined with cognitive empathy, it can create more of a problem than a solution. In that case, the observer gets dragged into the emotional state of the other, not necessarily knowing the way out.

• *Compassionate empathy* drives selfless will to help others to deal with a situation.

When we experience a need, we seek different levels of involvement to meet it. The theoretical knowledge of the mechanism that drives emotions and the way people deal with them can help us make appropriate choices.

It is important to remember that there is a fundamental difference between sadness and clinical depression. Sadness is always triggered by a loss of something or somebody valuable or loved. Depression is an abnormal emotional state when one is feeling sad about everything. It is a severe clinical state, often accompanied by hormonal imbalance and changes in brain chemistry, and requires corresponding medical attention and care.

SUMMARY

We should accept sadness as a vital emotion that testifies to our capacity to care and to love. Shared sadness facilitates bonding and strengthens relationships. If you are experiencing sadness, try to pay attention to your state and the stages you go through.

Don't be afraid to ask for help, but choose who and when you ask mindfully. We cannot expect empathy from everyone. People who deal with the emotional distress of others on a daily basis, like policemen, medical doctors, veterinarians, judges, and the like would be potentially hampered at their jobs if they were to get emotionally involved with every case they deal with.

At the same time, we should stop telling people that they shouldn't be sad. Independently of our involvement, we should ensure them instead that their state is absolutely normal and understood.

Furthermore, for people who are close to us, we need to show empathy—to go down for them in a cave of their sadness and walk them back toward the light.

CHAPTER 9
TRICKY PLEASURES

Society offers us various reasons to proceed with our lives, despite long odds. Starting from a Darwinist approach of survival of the species and followed by religious and spiritual traditions, there are many high-aim, long-term justifications for our existence. However, those reasons give controversial guidance for how we should fill our days, and they often honor limitations and suffering. At the same time, we must admit that positive emotional experiences, and the pleasures that facilitate them, make existence not only bearable, but enjoyable.

While our biology is adjusted for survival and thus tuned to better recognize negativity and danger, we all long to feel good. So how does feeling good work?

In general, the feeling of pleasure is controlled by hormones. Depending on external stimuli, endocrine glands inject the corresponding hormone into our blood. As with emotions, these mechanisms developed to support and stimulate our survival. Science describes four main pleasure hormones: dopamine, oxytocin, serotonin, and endorphin.

Dopamine developed to motivate us to reach our goals. It stimulates us to seek out what we want, even if it requires significant effort. Without it, we would have been unlikely ever climb up a tree to get a banana, cross the oceans, or invent tools. It gives us the joy of achieved reward, but only the first time. Dopamine has a stimulating nature that aims to boost our development. But it has its dark side: It always leaves us wanting more.

Oxytocin drives our social behavior, ensuring that we take care of our offspring. It is commonly called the "love hormone." The pituitary gland releases oxytocin at the moment we drop our defenses toward others and allows us to enjoy their closeness and touch. It's possible to say that it drives our feeling of trust toward others. We also experience oxytocin's effect when we pet a dog or feed a squirrel in the park. What's more, it was discovered that mammals with high oxytocin levels have a tendency toward monogamy. Thus, if you do not feel a predisposition to monogamy, oxytocin is a hormone you might be lacking.

Endorphin helps us to release physical and mental stress. It is a natural painkiller that gives us a short respite without pain, which might be crucial for survival before we realize an injury. We all experience the endorphin effect during genuine laughter. Equally important, it makes us feel good after an intense cry. Endorphin is associated with euphoria and the so-called "runner's high."

Serotonin facilitates our need for dominance and security, including finding a safe location and access to vital resources. It is linked to the emotion of contempt that manifests our superior position towards others.

Compared to millions of years of evolution, our lifestyle has changed dramatically in the last few thousands of years, and our biology hasn't had enough time to adjust yet. That is why some mechanisms that are supposed to better our lives sometimes work against us.

The ease with which we are able to satisfy our vital needs in today's age creates dissatisfaction, and the need for dopamine-type pleasure pushes us to desire unnecessary things. We don't need to hunt or search for our food anymore. Nowadays, most of us buy food in supermarkets, not often aware of where it comes from. Routines and habitual things do not stimulate a dopamine response, so we need to search for more and better.

Furthermore, in many parts of the world, this century has been an era of inflated consumerism. Advertisements now reach us wherever we are, through billboards, TV channels, smartphones, and even product packaging, screaming: "You need to have this to be cool, to be worthy, to be desired, to be recognized!" Society drives us full speed toward pleasant emotions almost exclusively out of contempt—needing to feel better than others.

Sports brands push us to compete with slogans like, "Impossible is nothing" and "Just do it." On the internet, brands follow you wherever you go, insisting: "Get it, get it." It is cooler! It is cheaper! It is a smarter deal! Here is the most expensive status thing everyone would envy! Only this will make you most desirable you. All of these ads are begging for two of our pleasure hormones: dopamine and serotonin, tricking us with a longing for reward, secure resources, and dominance.

Unfortunately, the lifestyle that is continuously advertised to us is more imaginary than realistic. Our inflated desires are not always achievable. Failing to establish a societal position according to unrealistic standards can lead to a lack of serotonin, which is directly linked to depressive conditions. And chasing after dopamine can lead to shopaholism, workaholism, gambling, and drug addiction.

The physical activity that helps us to release endorphins has also declined in the last century. No longer are we required to walk long distances, run, and lift heavy weights, since we have invented vehicles and machines to facilitate these activities. Nevertheless, we need to take at least ten thousand steps per day to maintain our mental and physical health. Maintaining an active lifestyle and playing sports, in particular, reduce the risks of depression, and have a positive effect on people who already suffer from it.

At the same time, technology separates us further from each other and from real human contact. We spend more time texting friends and family than meeting them in person, where we can touch them and experience closeness. It is more challenging to get the pleasure of the human touch than to click a *buy* button or communicate "frictionlessly" via electronics. But according to recent psychological research, we need at least eight hugs per day to maintain our well-being.

SUMMARY

Consciously or unconsciously, we all want to be happy and enjoy our time on earth. We all seek and long for pleasure. Just as there are no good or bad emotions, there are no better or worse pleasure hormones. They are all required, and we feel happy if they are in the right balance.

Try to identify your sources of pleasure and those you are missing. Aim to develop healthy habits of pleasure stimulation.

For dopamine: Define small steps toward your goals and recognize the accomplishments of them on a daily basis. Instead of possessing things, begin to enjoy the fruits of your own creation: begin to draw, take up carpentry or knitting, make pottery, and the like.

For oxytocin: Maintain warm relationships, hug your loved ones often. When you have an urgent need for oxytocin, go get a massage and enjoy fountains of it.

For serotonin: This is probably the most complicated hormone to get a boost of without appearing as an arrogant snob or applause-seeking fool. But it is not impossible. Serotonin releases when you are satisfied with who you are and are being recognized for your achievements. Pay attention to the positive impact you have on your family and the contributions you make at work. Stay tuned to appreciative nonverbal communication from others. Start to notice and compliment the achievements of others, and very likely they will respond with praise for yours.

For endorphin: Look for reasons to laugh. Don't miss a chance, unless it can appear offensive. Allow yourself a good cry now and then to release tension. And finally, do some physical activities. Choose a competitive sport; when you win, you'll get a serotonin boost as a bonus. Set small goals (pull more weight, run faster or longer distances) and you will get dopamine boost as a bonus.

CHAPTER 10
SPEAKING ABOUT EMOTIONS

The ability to express and describe emotions in words is important. First of all, putting feelings into words stimulates reflection on one's own emotional state, helping to define it. Furthermore, sharing feelings and emotions helps us bond and increases levels of intimacy in relationships, though the degree of openness depends on established levels of affinity between conversing individuals.

Research has established behavioral patterns that can help one recognize if people are conveying interest:

- They lean forward
- They orient their body more directly toward you
- They gaze at you more frequently
- They smile and nod more
- They increase the level of physical contact

If you don't observe any of the above-listed behaviors, it could be a signal that rapport between you and the other is not established.

When people get emotionally involved in a conversation, it shows by the following actions:

- They start to talk faster
- They pause less frequently
- They use a louder voice

• There is more variation in vocal pitch

As you can see, these behavioral patterns can be easily confused with the expression of anger, although it is the opposite of that: In this case, these behaviors signal that a person finds the conversation exciting and/or important.

We should not forget that disclosing our feelings exposes our weaknesses and makes us vulnerable in front of others, for who knows if they have bad or manipulative intentions? That is why it's useful to have a mental checklist of reasons why the person would be interested in a conversation on that level and how much they disclose in return.

Overall, finding the right balance of sharing your feelings and emotions is key to harmonious well-being in society.

A scientific study of the way we naturally use words to express emotions is quite challenging. For one, there are strong cultural and linguistic influences. Secondly, the fact of being observed increases awareness and may change natural behavior.

Until now, the best data and insight into this topic were from studies of verbal interactions between married couples. There, the goal is usually to resolve protracted, lasting conflicts, or to figure out the dynamic that leads to successful marriages.

Interestingly, studies have found out that women report that they express emotions more frequently than men. But objective observation does not confirm that, instead suggesting that both genders on average demonstrate the same emotional expressiveness.

But there is some evidence that women express more

hostile emotions about their partners, while men express less vulnerability and regret. Here it's easy to joke that both genders would look forward to experiencing precisely the opposite.

Most of our cognitive and conscious communication is ruled by the need to save *face*. Face is a concept for an individual's public self-image. It reflects the way we want to be perceived by others in our broader social environment. Sociologist Erving Goffman coined the term in 1960; since then, it has become widely used and studied in psychology, sociology, marketing, and many other areas, and explicated in the theory of politeness introduced by Brown and Levinson.

This concept was known in other languages and cultures before Goffman introduced it as a scientific term. For example, in English, we say, "Our boss hates to lose face in front of us when he gets reprimanded by the general manager." "Losing face" means to look bad in front of others. But the way we experience and perceive what "to look bad" means also differs.

Studying the face concept further, Brown and Levinson proposed a differentiation of positive and negative face and suggested that one or the other prevails in different cultures.

Positive face seeks for one's self-image to be appreciated and approved by others, while *negative face* looks for independence and freedom of action based on personal values, not values imposed by others.

Studies have shown that we usually try to have conversations in such a way that we collaborate with our interlocutor to maintain face. Unfortunately, if our face type and other cultural and idiosyncratic factors differ, we risk creating a face threat accidentally.

Let's imagine a lady with positive face in a shop. She sees on the top shelf a bag that attracts her attention, and she asks the shopkeeper to show it to her. The shopkeeper, who has negative face, knows that the bag is overpriced in comparison with other items. Appealing to the negative face of the lady, the shopkeeper suggests another bag, revealing that the one in question is too expensive. The positive-face shopper cares for the appreciation and approval of others, and, concluding that the shopkeeper identified her as not worthy of the expensive bag, gets deeply offended. That is an example how a good intention can go wrong.

Disclosures of emotions can be classified according to how much they honor or threaten the face-needs of the conversation partners. They can be face-honoring, face-compensating, face-threatening, or face-neutral.

With face-honoring emotions, we communicate to the other that their actions or appearance are appreciated or are a source of pleasure: "I'm so happy to see you," "I'm so proud of you," "You fill my heart with joy," "I was amazed by your speech," "I love you," and so forth.

Expressions of regret for misconduct toward the other are face-compensating: "I'm sorry," "I feel awful that it happened," "I'm so sad that I can't take back what I said," "I feel so guilty," and the like.

Face-threatening disclosures have more variations than others. They can expose our vulnerabilities, as for example: "I feel hurt," "I feel so helpless," "I'm so frustrated by this situation that I would just give up." They can also reveal a hostile state: "I'm so mad at you" or "It just makes me feel furious." Or they can reveal a feeling about what happened between a third person and us: "I feel ashamed for the way I treated him that day."

Face-neutral disclosures relate to our feelings about absent others: "I'm glad he finally passed exams," or "I'm angry that she didn't show up today." Sometimes they have nothing to do with an interpersonal relationship: "I always feel melancholy when it rains."

In conversation, we often have a choice of disclosing our vulnerability or expressing a threat to the face of the other.

When we say: *I feel* ___ (sad, unattractive, angry, scared, shocked, etc.), we expose ourselves in front of the other. We emanate openness and trust toward the other.

When we say: *You make me feel* ___ (sad, unattractive, angry, scared, shocked, etc.), we formulate our feelings as an accusation toward the other. We express the threat to the face of the other and can only expect self-defense.

Our emotional vocabulary also plays a significant role and can help us to express ourselves more accurately.

If you have difficulties describing how you feel, try to start from the seven universal emotions. In most cases, synonyms that describe emotions can represent intensity levels or blends.

Anger family: Annoyed --> Irritated --> Angry --> Mad --> Furious

Happy family: Amused --> Glad --> Joyful --> Happy -> Blissful

Frustration: anger plus sadness (as it represents an obstacle to a goal you can't overcome, and thus the beginning of accepting a loss).

Jubilation: signifies great happiness and triumph that

can be associated with contempt (as besides joy of achievement, it comes with beating others).

It's also important to distinguish between words that define feelings and emotional states versus words that describe an attitude.

Emotions and Feelings	Attitudes
Annoyed, Afraid, Awkward, Affectionate, Anxious, Alarmed, Amazed, Astonished, Amused	Agreeable, Affable
Bitter, Bashful, Blue, Baffled, Blissful	Brave, Bothered, Bold
Cranky, Cheerful, Content	Cooperative, Confident, Calm, Cold, Curious, Considerate, Cautious
Depressed, Discouraged, Delighted, Disgusted, Doleful	Disengaged, Distant, Daring, Determined
Embarrassed, Edgy, Excited, Envious, Exhausted, Enraged, Euphoric	Exuberant, Extravagant, Eager
Frightened, Fearful, Furious, Frustrated	Fair, Foolish, Funny, Forgiving,
Grumpy, Glad, Guilty, Gloomy	Generous, Greedy, Grateful, Grouchy
Heartbroken, Hysterical, Hopeless, Horrified, Hurt, Happy, Hateful	Hesitant, Humbled
Irritable	Interested, Insecure, Impatient, Inspired,

	Indifferent
Jealous, Joyful, Joyous, Jubilant	Judgmental, Jocular
	Kind, Keen
Lonely, Loved, Love	Lazy, Leery
Mad, Moody, Melancholic, Marvelous	Manipulative, Melodramatic, Mean
Nervous, Numb,	Naughty, Nasty, Neglectful, Needy, Naive
Obsessed, Offended, Outraged	Obedient, Optimistic, Open
Panicky, Peaceful, Proud, Peeved, Panicked	Playful, Pensive
	Quirky, Quarrelsome, Qualified, Quiet
Relieved	Rebellious, Reluctant, Reassured, Remorseful, Reserved, Rejuvenated, Restless, Rattled
Sad, Surprised, Scared, Sorrowful, Stressed	Shy, Satisfied, Sensitive, Safe, Stubborn, Sarcastic, Spiteful, Scornful, Secure, Skeptical
Terrified, Torn, Touched, Threatened	Tender, Tranquil, Timid,
Unhappy, Unsteady, Uplifted, Unsure, Uptight	
Vulnerable	Vivacious, Vain, Vibrant, Violent
Withdrawn, Worthless, Woeful, Worried, Worn	Wary, Wishful, Whimsical, Withdrawn

New technologies have allowed us to introduce emotional markers, so-called "emoticons" or "emojis," into our written speech. They are used in text messages, chats, social media posts, e-mails, and other written electronic channels.

Do emoticons help us add emotional charge to our written communication when people are not able to register nonverbal cues? From one point of view, they can help reduce ambiguity and reinforce a message's meaning. From another, emoticons are often emblematic, and not always scientifically accurate. Thus, they work better for people who have a shared understanding of emblematic meaning. But if that shared understanding is not established, emoticons can be misleading.

For example, the emoticon with a unilateral smile, which can be identified as contempt in the interpretation of 35–50-year-olds, signifies sarcasm to them. But younger people read it as a sign of flirtation.

Some emoticons represent emblematic hand gestures: OK, fingers crossed, palms together and so on. In different cultures those emblems may carry totally different, and sometimes offensive, meanings. It is important to keep that in mind to avoid ambiguous situations during cross-cultural communication.

What's more, the variety of emoticons we easily can send and interpret in the same way is quite limited and does not support the expression of subtle nuances or strengths. Paradoxically, that limits the way we express and identify our feelings.

SUMMARY

Although verbal communication seems to be under our full control, it is imperative to be mindful and attentive to others to ensure fruitful conversations are had at adequate levels of emotional disclosure.

Try the following exercises:

- Pay attention to how you deal with a face-threat.
- Try to register what type of emotional words you use and how often.
- Pay attention to whether you create a face-threat to others.
- When do you feel a need for emotional disclosure and how do you deal with that need?

CHAPTER 11
MEMORY

Memory is one of the most mysterious features in all living organisms. It encodes the ability to process and use information we have acquired from past experiences. That would be a straightforward subject if our memory worked in the same way as a computer's memory: brain gets an input, stores it, retrieves it at need. But memory mechanisms are much more sophisticated.

As this subject is very broad and complex, in this chapter I'll cover general terms and focus on areas related to emotions and communication.

Types of Memory

You may be at least somewhat familiar with the terms *short-term memory* and *long-term memory*. Short-term memory refers to our ability to remember information that we intend to use immediately: a phone number we want to call, the address of a restaurant we want to tell to a friend, the price of clothes we are considering buying, and so on. It is all about information that passes through our brain, often without need to be transformed into a long-term memory. It is very fragile and can easily vanish. I'm sure it has happened to you at least once that you were filling in forms, copying your passport or ID number, and you must keep checking and rechecking it while it slides away as you switch from task to another. Short-term memory lasts only for 15–30 seconds and has limited capacity. If you have ever tried to learn foreign language, you have been in a situation where you would look up a translation for the same word over and over again. If it doesn't transform into a long-term memory, it disappears very quickly.

Scientists disagree on the limitation of short-term memory. In 1956, George Miller introduced the "magic number 7 +/- 2" concept, which defines the capacity of a short-memory in which seven is the top limit of information chunks that can be remembered at once.

Nelson Cowan in 2001 summarized other research that cast doubt on Miller's definition and proposed a magic number of four.

To experiment, try to memorize the following sequence of numbers one by one as they are written:

1, 4, 7, 11, 6, 9, 5, 3, 8, 23

Look at it for a minute, close the book, and try to write down the sequence. Unless you have an extraordinary short-term memory, it will not be easy. Now try to memorize another sequence:

147, 116, 953, 823

That should be significantly easier, though it is exactly the same set of numbers, divided into fewer chunks.

In verbal communication, this type of memory doesn't play an important role, unless someone is talking to you and you are not really paying attention. In this case, short-term memory can save you when they ask, "What did I just say?"

Long-term memory is divided into implicit and explicit memory. *Implicit memory* is considered the most primitive and ancient type of memory; in a sense, it is shared with most animals and allows us to retain all the sensory motor coordination that we develop in life. It includes all sorts of skills: how to walk, how to eat with a spoon or chopsticks, how to ride a bike, to skate, to knit, and so on. This type of memory is also the most durable. Usually skills we learn once stay with us even if they are not practiced often. From the perspective of communication, this type of memory also doesn't play a role, unless you want to use it to make an impression on someone.

Explicit memory is subdivided into semantic and episodic memory.

Semantic memory is a repository of our general knowledge, such as names, animals, plants, books, countries and their capitals, specific terminology, and so forth. What role does it play in communication? We all tend to assume that we share the same vocabulary, and that facts that are obvious for us are equally obvious to others. In reality, of course, we all have different interests, are knowledgeable in different areas, and pay attention to different news.

The subjectiveness of semantic memory is especially important to keep in mind during cross-cultural communication, particularly when both parties communicate in a language not native to them or when language level differs. It is also important during work-related communication with clients or between different departments, where knowledge levels and specific terminology may be not obvious. If we do not ensure that information we are sending is received correctly, and if the other party hesitates to admit and clearly state certain knowledge gaps and follows their own limited assumptions of the meaning, it may lead to undesirable results.

Moreover, in our era of manipulative media and digital information that is full of the false and distorted facts, assumptions act as a barrier to fruitful communication by causing misinterpretations and misunderstandings. Instead of bringing us to the same page, they keep us far away from each other on islands of unconscious separation.

Episodic, or *narrative*, memory is the most interesting from the perspective of emotions and communication. We build up our vision of the world from a combination of semantic and episodic memory, while we almost fully rely on episodic memory when it comes to relationships. It develops between 18 and 30 months, which explains why we do not remember the very beginning of life.

How does episodic memory work? Why do we remember certain events and not others? Why do we memorize the same events differently compared to other people? How reliable are those memories? While science has some answers, this subject still has many blank spots.

Numerous studies have shown that the process of transforming our perceptions into long-term memories strongly depends on strengthening the connections between the neurons in the brain. That is accomplished by the frequent and repeated firing of pathways between neurons, known as *long-term potentiation*. The period of time in which long-term potentiation occurs and in which memories are stored is known as the period of consolidation. Consolidation of the memories formed during the day often happens during sleep.

That finding corresponds to the well-known

expression, "Let's sleep on it." Scientifically, it means, "Let our brain sort it out and consolidate the information we collected during the day to prepare a better basis for making decisions and/or reaching conclusions."

Narrative information about what happened to us or to others is encoded in our long-term memory if, during the episode, we experienced a higher than normal emotional charge. Examples include the first day of school, fishing with one's grandfather in perfect harmony, a first kiss, or a funny episode with friends.

For me, one of the most memorable episodes was my first rock climbing experience when, at age nine, I discovered that I'm terrified of heights.

When we recall a memory of something that happened to us, we usually believe that what we remember is exactly what happened. Funnily enough, we are often mistaken, sometimes greatly. Our episodic memory is reconstructive. That means that every time we recall a certain episode, we do not recall it as it happened in a reality—hours, days, months, or years ago—but we build it up all over again based on our previous recall of the episode. From recall to recall, our memories lose some details and gain others. If there was a funny episode that you keep telling your friends about, chances are it becomes more and more colorful in your memory and obtains details it didn't have during the first recall, in effect getting further away from the original event.

Most of us have a tendency to "fill in the blank spots" in a memory. If you are pushed to remember something but can't, you may unconsciously invent the answer that your brain considers most suitable. If someone asks you to recall in detail how a friend was dressed at a party, most likely you'll "remember" details that were never there. It also depends on how the question is formulated. If someone asks you, "What color was the car he left in?" you will think of a suitable color, meanwhile missing the fact that you haven't seen anyone leaving by car.

We often use our semantic memory to fill in the gaps in our episodic memory.

Paradoxically, while high emotions increase the chances of an episode becoming memorable, they also influence our perception in such a way that distorts reality and thus our memories as well.

For example, let's imagine you get really angry arguing with someone, and the argument doesn't get resolved at the time. You walk away from the situation still angry and keep turning it over in your thoughts. If you remember Chapter 3, when we are emotional our brain filters information in such a way that it feeds the emotion we are experiencing. The same effect happens to our memories. That is why dwelling on an unresolved angry episode that just happened often makes us even angrier. Moreover, the angry state can trigger a cascade of contextual memories. Those memories, which we may not even be aware of in our normal state, can suddenly surface, triggered by a similar context, be it a smell, view, emotional state, or similar.

That is why we often hear in fights between romantic couples a whole list of previous faults: "And also last month you weren't nice to my mother! And you made this joke about her at the party last year! And... And... And..." Our memory offers the full arsenal of arguments to stand for our anger rights.

That is also why the best strategy with angry episodes

that enter a vicious circle is to step out and distract yourself with something totally unrelated, until your amygdala calms down, allowing you to look at the situation rationally again. When you ensure that your opponent has calmed down as well, you can return to the conversation with a different, more mindful approach.

Finally, by the age of four, we develop *script memory*. This is a type of memory for how frequently repeated events happen. For example, a morning routine: I get up, take a shower, make a coffee, eat a quick breakfast, and go to work. It's easy to recognize when someone is using script memory because it is usually sequential and lacks specific details. If you ask a child about their day at school, and the story jumps from one fact to another, most likely the child is using episodic memory. If the story is smooth and shallow, most likely it's a sign of script memory.

In verbal communication, people often use script memory when they are not interested in your question or when they want to conceal something.

Apart from remembering and memorizing things, we also forget things, except for very exceptional cases of people who have been diagnosed with *hyperthymesia*: a phenomenon of exceptional long-term memory that is still not well understood by science. Normally, because of the reconstructive nature of explicit memory, we remember best those words, facts, and situations that we recall often. Metaphorically speaking, knowledge about other things still exists somewhere in the dusty shelves of our brain as neuron connections, but we are not even aware of it anymore.

Separate from this normal forgetting is *amnesia*—the

inability to recall something that most people should be able to recall. Amnesia is usually caused by an accident leading to concussion or other brain damage, or toxic poisoning as can result from excessive consumption of alcohol. *Anterograde amnesia* is an inability to maintain long-term memory concerning new events in life and is well demonstrated in the movie *Memento* (2000). *Retrograde amnesia* concerns loss of the memory before the incident.

There is a fine line between amnesia caused by traumatic experience and motivated forgetting. Some things that happen to us can be so emotionally difficult or unbearable that those memories get blocked out by the brain. The person resists any recall and, consciously or not, avoids any context that could potentially stimulate it.

That particular type of forgetting led to a new branch in psychology. It is believed that while the brain can suppress memories, the aftereffect of an incident can still cause debilitating psychological problems, such as anxiety, depression, posttraumatic stress disorder, or dissociative disorders. Because a person can't understand or explain to himself where these states originate, it enhances their negative effects. Thus, the idea of bringing those memories to normal consciousness is thought to improve and heal those unwanted conditions.

Attempts to find those "hidden" memories boosted yet another branch of psychological research, when Elizabeth Loftus helped reveal mechanisms that led to the creation of false memories.

We have already discussed false memories that we create for ourselves by enhanced and "improved" recall or by filling in memory gaps. But false memories can also be implanted in our brains, and it is quite a challenge not only for us but for all of neuroscience to figure out what is true and what is false. According to research, there is a correlation between vulnerability to the implantation of false memories and one's intelligence level. Nevertheless, if people we trust repeatedly ensure that certain plausible episodes happened to us, we will create those memories. In most of cases, it is not important and doesn't contain any danger for us since our brain is already full of false memories that we've created ourselves anyway. Unfortunately, false memories can be implanted with bad intention by manipulators and abusers. Often, victims who are isolated can lose connection with reality and have real difficulty figuring out what is true and what is enforced reality.

Nonetheless, the best part of memory's reconstructive nature is that we can recall positive and pleasant memories as often as we like and treat negative ones as a learning opportunity. Then our past will always remain on the light and happy side of life.

SUMMARY

Short-term memory:
- Contains information for immediate use
- Fragile
- Vanishes with a distraction

Implicit memory:
- Sensory-motor coordination
- Present at birth
- Mostly irrelevant in communicative and emotion

contexts

Semantic memory:
• Learned and therefore idiosyncratic
• Contains general knowledge
• May be involved in filling in episodic memory gaps

Episodic memory:
• Reconstructive and therefore not fully reliable
• Tends to focus on emotionally charged episodes
• Perceptional
• Depends on frequency of recall

Script memory:
• Represents reconstruction of routines
• Is an approximation of repeated past events

CHAPTER 12
STORIES ABOUT BIASES

Bias is yet another phenomenon that distorts the world around us, influences our perception, and governs our actions. But if we manage to become aware of our own biases, we can extend our perceived reality, giving ourselves the ability to handle life more deliberately.

The degree and variety of biases depend on personal history, tendencies, and predispositions. For example, if somebody grows up in a very peaceful and secure atmosphere, never experiencing mistreatment or betrayal, they would hardly expect people to behave otherwise and could miss potential cues for malicious intent. On the other hand, one who has experienced unfair treatment for a long period of time would be less likely to recognize the positive intentions of people toward them.

There are no better or worse biases, if we handle them mindfully.

The simplest example to illustrate this is the lie-versus-truth bias. There is hardly any human in the world who can claim to have a purely neutral position when it comes to trusting the words and actions of others. In an extreme example, some people will keep believing a lie against all evidence to the contrary. Others will doubt the "truth" even if all evidence supports it. Either bias can be harmful to our well-being and relationships unless we are aware of the tendency. As soon as we are conscious of it, we can make suitable adjustments to our behavior.

The best way to deal with biases is to keep in mind that whatever your assessment of the situation is, you might be wrong.

Let's consider some well-known, scientifically identified biases that we all share to a degree.

Attribution Bias

When we interact with people, even those whom we have known for a long time, we have no clear idea who they really are and what is going on inside their heads and hearts. Usually, we draw conclusions from what we see and experience ourselves. We observe someone's actions, hear their words, read nonverbal cues, but we can't truly know how a particular situation and recent events are influencing it.

The tendency to make judgments about the unique properties of a person on the basis of their actions that could be explained by contextual and external influence is called *correspondence bias* or *fundamental attribution error*.

For example, if we see a beggar on the street, we'd sooner believe that it's a lazy, unmannered person who doesn't want to work or study, often not questioning what life circumstances preceded their current condition and where those circumstances could lead us if we were in their place.

Because of a lack of empathy and a general inability to "walk in somebody else's shoes," we tend to believe that if the person has done something negative or ended up in a bad situation, it is in their character. But paradoxically, when we see other people's achievements and positive outcomes, we tend to attribute it to lucky situations or fortunate concurrences.

I bet you have thought or at least have heard from someone that "if I would get this or that opportunity, then I also would ____." The hard work, efforts, and character that carried a person through some difficulty are usually not as visible to us as their success, and we are not so eager to look for them. It is more comforting to believe in a lucky chance someone got than in the just rewards from hard work that we probably could be doing as well.

Meanwhile, thinking about ourselves, we tend to apply exactly the opposite measurements: we attribute our achievements to our personality and efforts, while blaming the situation when things go wrong.

As you can imagine, that creates miscommunication. When we search for understanding, we get blamed instead. And when we are proud of our achievements and hope for praise, we are just considered to be lucky.

While dealing with attribution biases, it is essential to keep in mind one thing: We don't know what others are going through, just as we cannot feel the "audience pressure" that exists in the mind of a public speaker.

Instead of jumping to conclusions based on information that is salient, it is useful to ask yourself what information is missing or invisible.

"Me" Theory

There is one person in the world you know and understand the most—yourself. That is why there is a propensity to draw conclusions about the words and actions of others based on how you see yourself in a similar situation.

Therefore, sometimes explanations and motivations of other people just do not make any sense.

"How can she do it? I would never..."

"I wouldn't get offended if..."

"It's impossible to do not realize that..."

"Who in their right mind would..."

Saying those things, we automatically assume that we have a right for our expectations regarding others based on what we think of ourselves.

But all people are different. We do not share the exact same knowledge, character, history, culture, fears, hopes, weaknesses, or values. Thus, in the same circumstances, we feel and act differently.

Moreover, research has demonstrated that often there is a significant difference between our attitude (what we believe we would do) and behavior (what we actually do) in a given situation. It is easier to stick to one's values and vision of good and bad in an imagined world, but things often change when we encounter reality and must act.

Confirmation Bias

Confirmation bias is what makes disputes go on forever and prevents us from taking arguments with objectivity. As soon as we have a particular belief or hypothesis, confirmation bias blinds us to any information that can shake or destroy it and makes us favorably interpret ambiguous information.

For example, if one partner has decided that the other is cheating, that partner will see shreds of evidence in every action, even if the conclusions contradict each other and do not follow any reasonable logic.

For instance: *"He didn't kiss me when he came home. He must be cheating"* and *"He kissed me when he came home because he is hiding that he is cheating."*

Our understanding of right and wrong and our self-positioning in the world are deeply linked to our entrenched beliefs. That is why anything that may compromise them appears as a direct threat to the core of our existence. Confirmation bias, in these cases, has the highest degree of influence. Religious beliefs, family values, romantic relationships, and culture-based norms are topics where confirmation bias often evades any reasoning and irrefutable facts.

Being ruled by confirmation bias, we can contravene logic, bending reality and adjusting the facts to fit our (possibly false) convictions. It not only affects the information-gathering process but it also makes our memory selective.

Predictably, confirmation bias is stronger in emotionally charged conversations. When you notice that your opponent is under the influence of confirmation bias and the atmosphere is heating up, the best strategy is to curtail the conversation before it goes too far.

To overcome our own confirmation bias, it is a good practice to have three hypotheses. If you have only two, it is easy to incline toward your preferred one, but having three creates a better logical balance.

For example, if, to come back to a cheating spouse, the hypothesis could be:

- She is cheating
- She is not cheating but hiding something else

- You are overreacting out of tiredness, boredom, and/or loneliness

In that way, there is a higher chance that your evaluation of evidence will be less biased toward your initial opinion.

Self-Fulfilling Prophecy and Behavioral Confirmation

Imagine a playground with a lot of children climbing, swinging, and running around. One of the mothers doesn't want her child to climb the high slide because she is afraid of him falling. She keeps repeating, "You shouldn't do it, you may fall badly!" Nevertheless, because all the other children are climbing the slide and her own child keeps insisting, she gives up. While the child is climbing, she keeps repeating, "Be careful, you are going to fall!" Finally, distracted and stressed, the child stumbles and the mother triumphs: "I told you!"

This is an example of a *self-fulfilling prophecy*, in which an initially false definition of a situation changes behavior, which makes the original false conception come true. Our own behavior can provoke conditions for something that wouldn't happen otherwise.

Imagine you have a long-lasting dispute with someone. You consent to make an attempt to come to an agreement. If, before the talk, you do not expect a positive outcome and arrive convinced that your opponent is not going to listen nor compromise, unconsciously you will behave according to this belief, pushing the opponent to follow the corresponding tone of the discussion. Obviously, this ensures that your expectations come true.

Another example of the self-fulfilling prophecy is the famous Pygmalion classroom experiment done by Harvard professor Robert Rosenthal in 1964. (It was repeated and confirmed multiple times.) At the beginning of the year, teachers would receive from a psychologist a forecast (entirely randomly assigned) about their students' abilities to dramatically exceed their performance by the end of the year. Biased by these predictions, teachers unconsciously would pay more attention to those children who were predicted to become high performers. Unsurprisingly, it resulted in an initial random prognostication to come true.

Self-fulfilling prophecy works in both directions, positive and negative. Imagine a situation at work in which you have weekly meetings with your manager. You believe that your manager appreciates you and you expect to be promoted. Hence, at every meeting, you are relaxed and friendly. You boast of your achievements, present failures as important opportunities for growth, and talk of grand plans. That creates a vibe that puts the development of the situation on the desired path.

Now imagine that you believe your manager doesn't like you. You are afraid of misjudgment. At every meeting, you are tense and defensive. You focus on justifying failures and forget to point out achievements. Instead of discussing plans, you talk about fears and possible pitfalls. That creates a corresponding vibe as well, shaping the situation and relationship accordingly. Nevertheless, while objectively your work successes and failures are the same in both cases, paradoxically it plays an insignificant role.

Obviously, you can find yourself on both sides of self-fulfilling prophecy and behavioral confirmation bias: being an influencer or being influenced by it.

Othello Error

The *Othello error* happens when we register information correctly but misinterpret its meaning. Paul Ekman initially proposed this term in his book *Telling Lies*, which uses the famous Shakespeare play as an example to explain this phenomenon. Othello believes in a false, fabricated accusation that his wife, Desdemona, has been cheating on him with another man. When he confronts her, he sees fear and distress, which he interprets as a reaction against disclosure, and thus confirmation of her guilt. On the basis of these nonverbal cues, Othello concludes that Desdemona's assurances of innocence are a lie, and he kills her. But the real reason for her behavior was her realization that she has no way to prove her innocence in the face of the aggressive behavior of her beloved husband. Misinterpreting the cues, fueled by confirmation bias, leads to a tragic outcome.

When you practice attentiveness to emotional cues, you will start to register more and more nonverbal information about the emotional states of people. At this point, it becomes essential to not fall into the Othello trap and remember that based on registered cues, you may be confident about the emotional state of others, but it doesn't mean you know the causes.

Cognitive Dissonance

Our brain doesn't like to deal with ambiguity. That is why when we consider contradictory ideas, beliefs, or values, the brain responds with discomfort and psychological stress. This is *cognitive dissonance.*

By 1959, Leon Festinger had concluded, based on a series of experiments, that if a person is induced to say or do something that is contrary to his private opinion, they tend to change or adjust their opinion to bring it to an acceptable level of correspondence to the requested action. That tendency is dictated by the need to solve cognitive dissonance.

Imagine a situation: A company general manager believes that people must be treated fairly and compensated accordingly for their contributions. Nevertheless, he has to fire a few people due to reorganization and budget restrictions. Moreover, the amount of compensation they can get is unfairly low. It is doubtful that he will change his initial belief about fair treatment because it is deeply linked to his values and the way he perceives himself. However, he can adjust his opinion about the qualities of the employees he needs to fire and of what compensation they deserve.

Cognitive dissonance is not always driven by external factors. Let's imagine a person who decides to quit smoking because it is ruining his health. Of course, his psychological and physiological dependence on smoking is still strong. So the person has a cigarette. This action contradicts with an initial intent to quit. Naturally, the person will find a justification why is it acceptable: "It's the last one" or "I have to reduce gradually." For that moment, it is a solution to cognitive dissonance. Now, imagine the person takes yet another cigarette, and another, until returning to the old smoking habit. The previous adjustment doesn't facilitate a solution anymore, so the person will need to make yet another adjustment. For example: "I would rather live a shorter life, but enjoy it the way I want."

Similarly, a person who while on a diet cannot resist a slice of cake will make a mental adjustment to solve cognitive dissonance. For example: "Today I had a tough day at work, so I need to let go, because otherwise, the situation exceeds my level of acceptable stress."

We resolve cognitive dissonance out of necessity to reduce mental stress. This influences our perception of our own decisions and actions, which means we must always find a way to reconcile it with our values and beliefs. In other words, it's not only our values that define our actions but also our actions that shape values. While those adjustments may work perfectly for us and our conscience, the way they are perceived by others often differs.

SUMMARY

Some biases have individual character. A particular group of people may have shared bias. Few biases are recognized as typical for most humans.

To practice awareness of your own biases, start to pay attention to them, starting from common biases described in this chapter:

• Observe your attribution patterns. Try to register the moments when you fall for confirmation bias and try to operate with three hypotheses.

• Observe your own behavioral confirmation patterns and those in your environment. Analyze them and try to come up with positive self-fulfilling prophecy strategies.
• Try to pay attention to the moments of cognitive dissonance and the way you solve them.

CHAPTER 13
THE INVISIBLE INTERLOCUTOR

There is one person who remains invisible to you in every conversation you have. This person? It's you.

Have you ever paid attention to or tried to imagine how you appear while talking, and what sort of nonverbal signals you are sending to people? Have you ever analyzed how those signals and appearances influence the perception of the information you are conveying? And what kind of behavioral confirmation bias they may create? Whether you paid attention or not, the influence is enormous.

We all recognize that appearance is important. We pay attention to how we dress, shaping the image we want to transmit to others with our clothes, accessories, hair, and makeup. We can consciously prepare it, check it in the mirror, and bring it to our total awareness.

But appearance is just a precondition, the point from whence the journey of communication starts. And when it starts, it simultaneously transmits information through these five channels.

Facial Expressions

As we discussed in previous chapters, it takes a fraction of a second for any emotion to appear on your face. Depending on the skills, sensitivity, and attentiveness of your interlocutor, the emotion can be processed on a cognitive or unconscious level. However, rarely does it pass completely unnoticed. And there is always a risk that it can be interpreted incorrectly.

Let's say a conversation you are having triggered a memory. That memory triggered an emotion. The emotion flashed across your face. Someone you are talking to cannot be aware of what is going on in your mind, and thus may falsely associate it to himself or to what has been said. But if you are aware of what happened, you can always explain yourself if necessary.

We also use facial expressions to show how we, or somebody we are talking about, felt in the past. For example, if you tell a story about a surprise party you organized for a friend, you may use a corresponding facial expression to show your friend's reaction.

The particularity of your face may create a perception of emotional expression. For example, lowered lip corners in a relaxed state may be confused with sadness. The particularity of eyebrows may make you look gloomy, sad, or surprised. Admittedly, it's hard, if not impossible, to change, and it isn't necessary to do so. But being aware of the particularity of your face can help ensure that your expressions are not being misinterpreted.

Body Language

We speak different body languages, depending on our character, temper, cultural background, and family norms. While some people may use a lot of gestures to illustrate speech, others remain motionless. While some have a particular sensitivity to personal space, others freely cross imaginary borders, getting close and seeking contact. We all use various manipulators: unconscious movements that help reduce nervousness or stress, such as rubbing hands, playing with hair, tensing the toes, biting the lip.

Our posture and body movements reveal a lot of personalized information. Either we feel energetic or tired, dominant or shy, confident or uncertain, open or distant, passive or aggressive, nervous or relaxed, and so on. It's possible to say that our body language has the most significant influence on how comfortable or uncomfortable others feel in our presence.

Voice

The strangest thing about our voice is that we hear it differently than others. If you ever have listened to your voice recorded, I bet it seemed odd and unfamiliar. However, vocal timbre is so unique that we can distinguish each other by it. While some characteristics of the voice remain constant, volume and pitch vary depending on our emotional state and intentions.

But even our baseline voice can have a substantial influence on how others perceive us. For example, somebody with a naturally high-pitched voice may be perceived as annoying or tiring because a high pitch signals fear, which may be unconsciously rendered as a warning and can keep people in alarm mode. At the same time, a high-pitched voice may also be perceived as a sign of fragility and induce a need to protect the speaker.

One friend of mine has a very loud voice. That could be very useful if he were singing opera or leading a revolution. However, in daily life, strangers often perceive it as a sign of aggression. Similarly, somebody with a quiet voice can be perceived as shy or weak.

Hence, awareness of own voice can help us to adjust to a particular context to not break norms and manage the impression we make.

It is also important to remember that physiological characteristics are misleading and should not be related to personality traits.

Verbal Style

Unlike the voice, verbal style is related to personality, language, and cultural background.

We speak at different speeds. We pause, use particular jargon and "parasite," or filler, words. Our speech can include stuttering and repetitions. Besides the natural baseline, all these factors may change during a conversation, revealing our cognitive load, doubts, uncertainties, equivocation, and emotional state.

Verbal Content

The words we choose to express ourselves with and the way we build up sentences also play a substantial role in how we communicate. For example, when someone says something is "important," they are choosing that word instead of "essential," "necessary," "indisputable," or many other synonyms. The word choice reveals our attitude toward the subject.

Our speech can be direct or indirect. We can say, "Close the door," directly expressing our will. Or we can say, "Don't you think it's cold with the door open?" assuming that our desire for the door to be closed will be understood.

Or we can form an accusatory sentence: "You didn't close the door," expecting the "mistake" to be corrected. Unsurprisingly, the reaction may not be always adequate to our expectations, especially if we make unrealistic judgments and assumptions about other people's knowledge of context.

In every interaction with others, we transmit information through five communication channels. While our body language and facial expressions are invisible to us, they are exposed to anyone who interacts with us. Furthermore, while we can hear our own tone of voice and words that we choose to express our thoughts and feelings, we often fail to pay close attention to them.

Nevertheless, consciously or unconsciously, wholly or partially, others register this information and form their impressions. Correctly or not, people make judgments concerning what they see and hear.

Paying attention to all five communication channels from others is a big challenge requiring practice. Paying attention to our own communication channels can be even more difficult, but also more rewarding. Luckily, we don't need to maintain this focus at all times. But it is essential to be able to make this evaluation in case the signals and feedback you register from others are not aligned with your expectations.

It's good to remember that tiredness, lack of sleep, and other various environmental distractions limit our attentiveness and ability to be continually present in the moment. That is why it's better to postpone important talks in such conditions, especially if a conversation becomes heated.

SUMMARY

We are invisible to ourselves in our interactions with others. But we can develop awareness to help get a better understanding of how other people perceive the signals we transmit through the five communication channels.

For example, if we see that our dress code doesn't fit a situation, we have to bear with it because it is not easy to change from the moment to another. If we pay attention to the way other people react to us, we can adjust quickly. It just requires willingness and practice.

I would like to suggest a few exercises:

1. Start from observing others to get a better understanding of interpersonal dynamics and the role of nonverbal communication.

Try to observe people in a cafe or restaurant:

- What is the body language dynamic?
- What emotions are they experiencing?
- What emotions are they trying to hide?
- Do they consciously notice nonverbal signals from each other?
- How does that influence the atmosphere between them?

Try this exercise at your workplace and home, too.

2. To develop self-awareness, start by paying attention to only one of the communication channels. At every conversation begin paying attention to your mimic (body language, voice, verbal style, verbal context) and register how it is influencing the discussion. Slowly it will become automatic and will not require special effort.

CHAPTER 14
EMOTIONALLY CHARGED
CONVERSATIONS

Besides daily communication, small talk, and casual discussion, we all now and then have tough conversations regarding a specific situation or with a particular person, the idea of which can make us emotional. For example:

- Apologies we want to make
- Meeting with someone who wants to apologize
- Sensitive issues we want to or have to address
- Parents solving problems between kids
- Favors we need to ask from uncooperative people
- Attempts to resolve prolonged family conflicts
- High-stakes negotiations with colleagues or partners
- Hiring and firing employees

We engage in emotionally charged dialogue more often than we may realize. Sometimes we find ourselves in these sorts of conversations being mentally unprepared to engage in them. Following a framework can help you successfully navigate difficult conversations, where the goal is to achieve mutual understanding and positive resolution. It consists of four stages:

Preparation

When we consider having a talk we expect to be challenging, an internal dialogue starts rolling in our mind. We mentally appeal to this hypothetical person, formulating what we would like to say. While this internal conversation unfolds, we get emotional, even before facing the real situation.

As much as this process can be constructive to formulate our thoughts, it can be destructive, as well. During these internal dialogues, we risk strengthening our biases and limiting our vision of the situation to only one side—our own.

So what does it mean to get prepared? You first need to formulate your goal by answering the following questions:

• What information do you want to convey to the other person?
• What do you want to achieve?
• What would be a successful resolution for you? Is it win–win? Win–lose? Other?
• What compromises are you willing to make, if any?

It is essential to formulate the goal because it will help you to maintain focus during the conversation, especially when emotions get triggered. This focus also prevents the other person from avoiding the topic of your interest and turning the conversation in a different direction.

Secondly, you need to analyze the person you are going to have a conversation with, the relationship you share, and their stakes in what you are trying to achieve. You can start by answering the following questions:

• Who is this person? What is their age, gender, current life situation, vocabulary and communication style, and personality? What are their values, beliefs, and interests?

• Do you share a relationship with a relevant third party, or a common attachment (such as to a colleague or a parent)?

• What in your attitude or communication style can appear as unpleasant or destructive to this person?

• Do you have emotional scripts that are related to the topic you are going to discuss or to this person in particular? What can trigger them?

• Are you aware of or able to identify the other person's emotional scripts related to you or to the subject at hand?

• Do you know the motives that drive the person?

• Do you know the interest and involvement of the person in the topic you plan to discuss?

• In case it is not the first attempt to have this conversation, what were the hotspots that made the talk go wrong previously, and how could you avoid them this time?

• What reaction do you expect from the person, and what compromises are you ready to make?

• What would be a good time and place for this conversation and why?

• Who is in charge of proposing and organizing the conversation and what would be a good format?

When all of these questions are answered, you can formulate the structure of your talk. Sometimes you may conclude that attempting to have it at this point in time is meaningless, because your goal is not realistic or cannot be reached under current circumstances. In that case, you can save time and nerves.

Comprehension

At the very beginning of a conversation, before getting to the core of it, try to establish rapport. Your opening line will determine the course of the conversation. Thus, make sure that it radiates openness, kindness, and sincere interest.

Introduce the topic and the goal you want to achieve. Sometimes it is helpful to explain your reasoning behind it. When that is settled, allow your interlocutor to express their point of view on the situation. You can introduce it with an open question:

- How do you feel about it?
- What is your opinion?

Do not interrupt and pay attention to:

- Your own five communication channels
- The five communication channels of your interlocutor
- Whether your emotional state is changing; if it does, register the triggers and try to calm it down with rational thinking

By the end of this stage, you should be able to address the following concerns:

- What is the perspective of your interlocutor?

• What do they see as a successful resolution?
• Formulate three hypotheses regarding unclear or especially sensitive questions

Clarification and Negotiation

This is the most critical stage. Here you enter the phase where all the cards are on the table, and you start working on moving toward the resolution. Here you need to verify the hypotheses that you formulated for yourself in the previous stage. Validate the credibility of the statements and start drafting the final conclusion of the conversation.

It's important to pay attention to your style of questioning. Open-ended questions help you gather more information, as they require more than one-word answers. Some examples:

"How did the fight between the two of you start?"
"What do you think would be a good solution?"
"What is your best memory of this period?"

Closed questions can be answered with "yes" or "no" and in some situations hasten the end of the conversation:

"Is that your final answer?"
"Should I call her and sort things out?"
"Did you do what I asked you to?"

For effective conversation, it is useful to avoid the following:

Leading Questions

This type of question carries your biases and leads others to give you an implied answer, often resulting in false or slanted information.

"Do you have any problems with your colleague?" This question implies that there must be some problem and prompts the person to question the relationship. The open way of asking the question would be: "Tell me about a relationship with your colleague."

"Do you seriously think this vase should belong to you?" This question not only carries a bias about the opinion of the other person but it also transmits a negative attitude concerning this opinion. That combination can drive strong negative feedback. A better way of getting information about the person's reasoning would be asking, "Who do you think grandma would like to have this vase and why?"

"How hard did he smash Brian?" Here, the word "smash" already assumes major damage. The better way to get information would be to ask: "What happened after Brian said that?"

"Did you stop getting wasted every evening?" This is an example of a leading closed question, where one is trapped into admitting being wasted in the past, whether or not they continue to do so. The better format would be: "How do you spend your evenings lately?"

Option Questions

This type of question forces a choice and limits the possibility of getting the truth or a different outcome:

"So, was it Brian or Dennis who started the fight?"

"Will you agree to this offer or will we proceed through

the courts?"

Marathon Questions

This is when we ask many questions in a row without allowing another person to answer. First, it puts too much of a cognitive load on the other person who would be trying to keep all the information in their short-term working memory. Secondly, it allows the other person to choose which question to answer and which to skip.

Pauses

Pauses play an essential role in communication. They signal to the other person that we have finished talking, and now they can contribute to the conversation or reply to our request. But we often have a natural intolerance to prolonged pauses; when our interlocutor keeps silent for more than a few seconds, usually we start talking again, providing more arguments or questions. This approach may disturb the thinking process of the other person or allow them to dodge the main question. Try to not interrupt pauses, no matter how long it takes for the other person, and you will discover magical benefits rewarding your patience.

During negotiation, you should always keep your goal in mind, bring the conversation back on track if it starts to deviate, and try to steer it to a successful resolution.

Resolution

To finish the conversation successfully, we need to verify that a mutual understanding has been reached, and everyone has the same perception of the state and any potential follow-up.

Before closing the conversation, answer for yourself the following questions:

- Have you communicated all you intended to?
- Did you reach your initial goal?
- Do you need to modify your initial goal according to compromises that were made?

After that, it is useful to summarize once again all the agreements and confirm actions that require follow-up.

SUMMARY

Successfully navigating emotionally charged conversations is a skill requiring a lot of work and practice. It may look overwhelming, but if you start gradually working on mastering your conversation style by developing awareness, you will begin to notice how it improves automatically. Don't try to embrace everything at once. In every conversation, choose one thing you will pay attention to with the aim of adjusting or improving it. That could be your emotional state, questioning style, or body language. When you feel confident, start to develop further.

The best words to summarize this chapter belong to Stephen Covey, author of the book *The Seven Habits of Highly Effective People*: "Seek first to understand, and then be understood."

CHAPTER 15
THE HARMONY OF EMOTIONAL BEING

According to much research, we are biologically attuned to perceive negativity more strongly than positivity. This is entirely logical from a survival point of view: We need to recognize half a million shades of bitter to avoid poisoning; we need a strong impulse for a fight-or-flight response triggered by anger or fear. On the whole, among universal emotions we can find only one undoubtedly positive against five that are somewhat negative, and one neutral. But all seven emotions may be perceived as pleasant depending on the person or situation. Research shows that to neutralize one negative sensation, we need to experience three to five positive ones. We have to find those positive emotions somewhere. But nobody teaches us how to do it or how to be conscious of it.

Starting from childhood, we learn to suppress our emotions, adjust to social demands, and substitute our dreams with what is convenient. We are continuously bombarded by imperative suggestions of what is expected from us and what is good for us. Specific examples depend on family, social level, culture, and other external factors, but the animating trend remains constant: If our dreams do not match conventional norms, we are encouraged to drop or postpone them. This limitation on the right to be yourself and to live your life according to an intuitive choice of a happy path soon becomes a lifestyle. We begin to eschew facing our real wishes and dreams to avoid the painful experience of letting them go. We stop thinking about what makes us happy, instead focusing on minimizing unhappiness.

Psychologists in the 19th and 20th centuries—Sigmund Freud in particular—defined the core of psychological stability as an ordinary misery. That is why we intuitively seek pleasures to fill in gaps: We overeat ice cream and cake, buy things we absolutely do not need, have random sex, and do a number of other sublimating actions, because we are not used to asking ourselves what really makes us happy, and simply try to do things that make us feel less miserable.

Our inner world turns messy and full of garbage and it becomes difficult to find ourselves in there. It is full of routines, gossip, fake news, prejudice, advertisements, goals that are not necessarily ours, and unprocessed emotions. Technology has sped up the world around us, reducing distances and allowing for travel and communication to happen incredibly fast compared to years past. At the same time, it introduced a lot of noise. And it made us always reachable, via messages, social media, phone calls, and other sources of electronic communication. By creating an illusion of closeness, the shrinking world has made relationships shallower and filled in the open spaces with metaphorical trash.

It has become difficult to find the time and courage to stay in touch with yourself, reflecting on your thoughts and needs, forming dreams that are truly yours and not proffered by society, avoiding being trapped by advertisements.

We need to learn to stop and take the time to look around and inside. We need to learn to pay attention and clean up the spaces inside and around us from unnecessary things. We need this space to get clarity and light, the same as you experience when opening the windows in a clean, fresh, empty room in the early morning.

We are getting used to living in a rush to be able to catch up with social expectations. Meanwhile, science is turning to ancient wisdom to study practices and techniques that allow us to find peace and harmony.

The first researcher to report the effects of meditation on brain structure was Harvard neuroscientist Sara Lazar (Massachusetts General Hospital). Using magnetic resonance imaging (MRI), she looked at the brain cortex—the outermost surface of the brain that plays a key role in memory, attention, perception, and consciousness. Typically, the cortex atrophies with age. In her experiment, Dr. Lazar found that the cortices of the research group that had years of meditative experience were thicker than those of a control group. In fact, that thickness corresponded to the width of nonpractitioners who were 20 years younger. She also observed differences in the brain area associated with sensation and emotion, empathy and love.

The latest research shows beneficial changes in brain structure can already occur after eight weeks of regular meditation. Moreover, that time of silence and purity can trigger beneficial changes in our overall self-perception.

We need to incorporate mindfulness in our lives to get nonjudgmental clarity on what is going on around us and allow us to find our own path to happiness.

When we are able to see clearly the current moment without distractions—when we do not rush with our thoughts in the future or stuck in the past—we live fully. We allow ourselves to notice details and the depth of being. We notice the emotions of people who surround us. That awareness expands our perception of the world, and gives us better choices for how to deal with it:

- Use our anger constructively and not destructively
- Manage fears better
- Ask for help
- Give a hug and support to those who need
- See and share the beauty and joy of being

Positive psychology argues against that acceptance of ordinary miscry, defining happiness as a deep satisfaction with life. I believe that this satisfaction is obtained through the harmony and balance of emotional being.

Happy people do not envy, do not start wars, and do not seek for the enslavement of earth's population to get money and resources.

My wish for you, dear reader, is to choose to learn to be happy—today, right now. Search and find in yourself the beauty, love, and kindness that is there. I hope this book has opened for you the door to your inner world, and is the beginning of a great journey.

*If you have questions about the book or related workshops, reach out to **tatiana@mindtwist.co***

ACKNOWLEDGEMENTS

This book is a significant accomplishment, and I would like to thank the people who opened this path for me, who motivated and supported me along the way.

I would like to thank my family for all the patience, time, and space they provided me with to focus on this work. Elio Cecchetto, Anastasia Cecchetto, Paris Bratsos—thank you for being my first readers and critics. Thank you, Alexandra Cecchetto, for all the hugs and care that kept me going at moments of tiredness.

Thank you very much Marc X. Makkes and Pascal Comvalius for the feedback, suggestions, and endorsement that helped me to improve these chapters.

Many thanks to Bartosz Kiera for telling me that it's time to write this book and for all the encouragement and support.

My enormous gratitude to Joseph Pelrine, who introduced me to the intriguing science of the human mind and supported me along the way.

I would like to thank Professor Dawn Archer, Aaron Garner, Cliff Lansley, and Dr. Samuel Larner for sharing their knowledge, answering millions of my annoying questions, and for keeping me challenged for many years of studies.

Many thanks to Poki B.V. and all the people who believed in me and supported me with pre-orders.

Special thanks to Natalia Pozdnyakova for being such an amazing and inspiring friend.

And finally, thanks to all the readers for investing your time in reading these chapters. I hope it was an intriguing journey.

SCIENCE BEHIND THE SCENES (FOR CURIOUS AND SUSPICIOUS MINDS)

Agrawal, N., & Maheswaran, D. (2005). The effects of self-construal and commitment on persuasion. *Journal of Consumer Research, 31*(4), 841–849. doi:10.1086/426620.

Alloy, L., & Riskind, J. (n.d.). *Cognitive vulnerability to emotional disorders.*

Altman, D. (2010). *The mindfulness code: Keys for overcoming stress, anxiety, fear, and unhappiness.* Novato, CA: New World Library.

Bachorowski, J., & Owren, M. (1995). Vocal expression of emotion: Acoustic properties of speech are associated with emotional intensity and context. *Psychological Science, 6*(4), 219–224. Retrieved 16 July 2017 from http://dx.doi.org/10.1111/j.1467-9280.1995.tb00596.x

Baddeley, A. D. (1986). *Working memory.* Oxford, UK: Clarendon Press. [aNC, ADB, SG, SM, BR, BJS, TS, rNC]

Baddeley, A. D. (1993). Visual and verbal subsystems of working memory. *Current Biology, 3,* 563–565. [BJB]

Baddeley, A. D. (1996). Exploring the central executive. *Quarterly Journal of Experimental Psychology, 49*A, 5–28. [ADB]

Baddeley, A. D. (2000). The episodic buffer: A new component for working memory? *Trends in Cognitive Sciences, 4,* 417–423. [ADB]

Baddeley, A. D. (in press). Levels of working memory. In M.

Naveh-Benjamin, M. Moscovitch, & H. L. Roediger (Eds.), *Perspectives on human memory and cognitive aging: Essays in honor of Fergus Craik.* [rNC]

Baddeley, A. D., & Ecob, J. R. (1973). Reaction time and short-term memory: Implications of repetition effects for the high-speed exhaustive scan hypothesis. *Quarterly Journal of Experimental Psychology, 25,* 229–240. [JJ]

Baddeley, A. D., Grant, S., Wight, E., & Thompson, N. (1975). Imagery and visual working memory. In P. Rabbit & S. Dornic (Eds.), *Attention and performance V.* London, UK: Academic Press. [ADB]

Banziger, T., & Scherer, K. (2005). The role of intonation in emotional expressions. *Speech Communication, 46*(3-4), 252–267. Retrieved from http://dx.doi.org/10.1016/j.specom.2005.02.016 [Accessed 17 July 2017].

Beaulieu, C. M. J. (2004). Intercultural study of personal space: A case study. *Journal of Applied Social Psychology, 34,* 794–805

Borg, C., & de Jong, P. (2012). Feelings of disgust and disgust-induced avoidance weaken following induced sexual arousal in women. *PLoS ONE, 7*(9), e44111. Retrieved 23 March 2019 from http://dx.doi.org/10.1371/journal.pone.0044111

Brown, P., & Levinson, S. C. (1987). *Politeness: Some universals in language usage.* Cambridge, UK: Cambridge Univ. Press.

Breuning, L. (2016). *Habits of a happy brain.* Avon, MA: Adams Media.

Brown, P., & Levinson S. C. (1978). Universals in language usage: Politeness phenomena. In E. Goody (Ed.),

Questions and politeness (pp. 56–310). Cambridge, UK: Cambridge University Press.

Brody, L. (1985). Gender differences in emotional development: A review of theories and research. *Journal of Personality, 53*(2), 102–149. Retrieved 18 July 2017 from http://dx.doi.org/10.1111/j.1467-6494.1985.tb00361.x

Buhlmann, U., Etcoff, N., & Wilhelm, S. (2006). Emotion recognition bias for contempt and anger in body dysmorphic disorder. *Journal of Psychiatric Research, 40*(2), 105–111. Retrieved 29 August 2017 from http://dx.doi.org/10.1016/j.jpsychires.2005.03.006

Cahill, L., & McGaugh, J. (1998). Mechanisms of emotional arousal and lasting declarative memory. *Trends in Neurosciences, 21*(7), 294–299. Retrieved 23 March 2019 from http://dx.doi.org/10.1016/s0166-2236(97)01214-9

Chopik, W. J., O'Brien, E., & Konrath, S. H. (2016). Differences in empathic concern and perspective taking across 63 countries. *Journal of Cross-Cultural Psychology, 48*(1), 23–38. doi:10.1177/0022022116673910.

Chronaki, G., Hadwin, J., Garner, M., Maurage, P., & Sonuga-Barke, E. (2014). The development of emotion recognition from facial expressions and non-linguistic vocalizations during childhood. *British Journal of Developmental Psychology, 33*(2), 218–236. Retrieved Accessed 18 July 2017 from http://dx.doi.org/10.1111/bjdp.12075

Cloninger, S. (2009). *Theories of personality*. Upper Saddle River, NJ: Pearson/Prentice Hall.

Covey, S. (2005). *The 7 habits of highly effective people.*

London, UK: Simon & Schuster.

Cowan, N. (2001). The magical number 4 in short-term memory: A reconsideration of mental storage capacity. *Behavioral and Brain Sciences, 24*(1), 87–114. Retrieved 23 March 2019 from http://dx.doi.org/10.1017/s0140525x01003922

Davis, D., & Hayes, J. (2011). What are the benefits of mindfulness? A practice review of psychotherapy-related research. *Psychotherapy, 48*(2), 198–208. Retrieved 23 March 2019 from http://dx.doi.org/10.1037/a0022062

Damasio, A. (1999). *The feeling of what happens: Body and emotion in the making of consciousness.* New York, NY: Harcourt Brace.

Darwin, C. (1872). *The expression of emotions in man and animals.*

Durlak, J., Weissberg, R., Dymnicki, A., Taylor, R., & Schellinger, K. (2011). The impact of enhancing students' social and emotional learning: A meta-analysis of school-based universal interventions. *Child Development, 82*(1), 405–432. Retrieved 30 July 2017 from http://dx.doi.org/10.1111/j.1467-8624.2010.01564.x

Ekman, P., & Friesen, W. V. (1978). *Facial Action Coding System: A technique for the measurement of facial movement.* Palo Alto, CA: Consulting Psychologists Press.

Ekman, P. (1992). Facial expressions of emotions: New findings, new questions. *Psychological Science, 3*, 34–38.

Ekman, P. (2006). *Darwin and facial expression.* Cambridge, MA: Malor Books.

Ekman, P. (2007). *Emotions revealed*. New York, NY: Henry Holt.

Ekman, P. (2009). *Telling lies*. New York, NY: W.W. Norton.

Feeser, M., Fan, Y., Weigand, A., Hahn, A., Gartner, M., Aust, . . . Grimm, S. (2014). The beneficial effect of oxytocin on avoidance-related facial emotion recognition depends on early life stress experience. *Psychopharmacology*, *231*(24), 4735–4744. Retrieved 28 August 2017 from http://dx.doi.org/10.1007/s00213-014-3631-1

Fernandez, G. (1999). Real-time tracking of memory formation in the human rhinal cortex and hippocampus. *Science*, *285*(5433), 1582–1585. Retrieved 23 March 2019 from http://dx.doi.org/10.1126/science.285.5433.1582

Guarnera, M., Hichy, Z., Cascio, M. I., & Carrubba, S. (2015). Facial expressions and ability to recognize emotions from eyes or mouth in children. *Europe's Journal of Psychology*, *11*(2), 183–196. doi:10.5964/ejop.v11i2.890.

Harrison, A., Tchanturia, K., & Treasure, J. (2010). Attentional bias, emotion recognition, and emotion regulation in anorexia: State or trait? *Biological Psychiatry*, *68*(8), 755–761. Retrieved 29 August 2017 from http://dx.doi.org/10.1016/j.biopsych.2010.04.037

Jung, H., & Yoon, H. (2016). Why is employees' emotional intelligence important? *International Journal of Contemporary Hospitality Management*, *28*(8), 1649–1675. Retrieved 23 July 2017 from http://dx.doi.org/10.1108/ijchm-10-2014-0509

Hazel, B., Lazar, S., Gard, T., Schuman-Olivier, Z., Vago, D., & Ott, U. (2011). How does mindfulness meditation work? Proposing mechanisms of action from a conceptual and neural perspective. *Perspectives on Psychological Science, 6*(6), 537–559. Retrieved 23 March 2019 from http://dx.doi.org/10.1177/1745691611419671

Hugdahl, K. (2001). *Psychophysiology*. Cambridge, MA: Harvard University Press.

Jha, A., Krompinger, J., & Baime, M. (2007). Mindfulness training modifies subsystems of attention. *Cognitive, Affective, & Behavioral Neuroscience, 7*(2), 109–119. Retrieved 23 March 2019 from http://dx.doi.org/10.3758/cabn.7.2.109

Kubler-Ross, E., & Kessler, D. (2005). *On grief & grieving: Finding the meaning of grief through the five stages of loss*. New York, NY: Scriber.

Ladd, G. W. (1990). Having friends, keeping friends, making friends, and being liked by peers in the classroom: Predictors of children's early school adjustment. *Child Development, 61*(4), 1081–1100. doi:10.1111/j.1467-8624.1990.tb02843.x.

Lane, R., & Nadel, L. (2002). *Cognitive neuroscience of emotion*. Oxford, UK: Oxford University Press.

Lazar, S., Kerr, C., Wasserman, R., Gray, J., Greve, D., Treadway, . . . Fischl, B. (2005). Meditation experience is associated with increased cortical thickness. *NeuroReport, 16*(17), 1893–1897. Retrieved from 23 March 2019 http://dx.doi.org/10.1097/01.wnr.0000186598.66243.19

Laukka, P., Juslin, P., & Bresin, R., (2005). A dimensional

approach to vocal expression of emotion. *Cognition and Emotion, 19*(5), 633–653.

Matthews, G., Roberts, R. D., & Zeidner, M. (2002). *Emotional intelligence: Science and myth*. Cambridge, MA: MIT Press.

LeDoux, J. E. (1996). *The emotional brain*. New York, NY: Simon & Schuster.

Loftus, E. F., Miller, D. G., & Burns, H. J. (1978). Semantic integration of verbal information into a visual memory. *Journal of Experimental Psychology, 4*, 19–31.

Liu, M., & Utama, N. (2014). Meditation effect on human brain compared with psychological questionnaire. *International Journal of Information and Education Technology, 4*(3), 264–269. Retrieved 23 March 2019 from http://dx.doi.org/10.7763/ijiet.2014.v4.410

Loftus, E. F. (1997). Creating false memories. *Scientific American, 277*(3), 70–75. doi:10.1038/scientificamerican0997-70

Loftus, E. F. (1979). The malleability of human memory: Information introduced after we view an incident can transform memory. *American Scientist, 67*(3), 312–320.

Masten, C., Guyer, A., Hodgdon, H., McClure, E., Charney, D., Ernst, M., . . . Monk, C. (2008). Recognition of facial emotions among maltreated children with high rates of post-traumatic stress disorder. *Child Abuse & Neglect, 32*(1), 139–153. Retrieved 29 August 2017 from http://dx.doi.org/10.1016/j.chiabu.2007.09.006

Matsumoto, D. (2005). Scalar ratings of contempt expressions. *Journal of Nonverbal Behavior, 29*(2), 91–104. Retrieved 29 August 2017 from http://dx.doi.org/10.1007/s10919-005-2742-0

Mayer, J., Roberts, R., & Barsade, S. (2008). Human abilities: Emotional intelligence. *Annual Review of Psychology, 59*(1), 507–536. Retrieved 23 July 2017 from http://dx.doi.org/10.1146/annurev.psych.59.103006.093646

Miller, G. (1994). The magical number seven, plus or minus two: Some limits on our capacity for processing information. *Psychological Review, 101*(2), 343–352. Retrieved 23 March 2019 from http://dx.doi.org/10.1037/0033-295x.101.2.343

Miller, R., & Matzel, L. (2006). Retrieval failure versus memory loss in experimental amnesia: Definitions and processes. *Learning & Memory, 13*(5), 491–497. Retrieved 23 March 2019 from http://dx.doi.org/10.1101/lm.241006

Myers, D. (2012). *Exploring social psychology*. New York, NY: McGraw Hill.

Myers, D., & Twenge, J. (2014). *Social psychology*. New York, NY: McGraw-Hill.

Morningstar, M., Dirks, M., & Huang, S. (2017). Vocal cues underlying youth and adult portrayals of socio-emotional expressions. *Journal of Nonverbal Behavior, 41*(2), 155–183. Retrieved 16 July 2017 from http://dx.doi.org/10.1007/s10919-017-0250-7

Pell, M., Paulmann, S., Dara, C., Alasseri, A., & Kotz, S. (2009). Factors in the recognition of vocally expressed emotions: A comparison of four languages. *Journal of Phonetics, 37*(4), 417–435. Retrieved 16 July 2017 from http://dx.doi.org/10.1016/j.wocn.2009.07.005

Paeschke A., Kienast M., Sendlmeier W.F. (1999). F_0-contours in emotional speech. *Proceedings of the*

International Congress of Phonetic Sciences (San Francisco, CA), *99*(2), 929–933.

Petrides, K. V. (2001). *A psychometric investigation into the construct of emotional intelligence* (Unpublished doctoral dissertation). University College London.

Petrides, K. V., & Furnham, A. (2003). Trait emotional intelligence: Behavioural validation in two studies of emotion recognition and reactivity to mood induction. *European Journal of Personality*, *17*(1), 39–57. doi:10.1002/per.466.

Riess, H. (2017). The science of empathy. *Journal of Patient Experience*, *4*(2), 74–77. Retrieved 23 March 2019 from http://dx.doi.org/10.1177/2374373517699267

Salovey, P., & Mayer, J. D. (1990). Emotional intelligence. *Imagination, Cognition and Personality*, *9*, 185–211.

Salovey, P., & Sluyter, D. (1997). *Emotional development and emotional intelligence*. New York, NY: Basic Books.

Sevinc, G., & Lazar, S. (2019). How does mindfulness training improve moral cognition?: A theoretical and experimental framework for the study of embodied ethics. *Current Opinion in Psychology*, *28*, 268–272. Retrieved 23 March 2019 from http://dx.doi.org/10.1016/j.copsyc.2019.02.006

Young, L., & Baime, M. (2010). Mindfulness-based stress reduction: Effect on emotional distress in older adults. *Complementary Health Practice Review*, *15*(2), 59–64. Retrieved 23 March 2019 from http://dx.doi.org/10.1177/1533210110387687

Yrizarry, N., Matsumoto, D., & Wilson-Cohn, C. (1998). American-Japanese differences in multiscalar intensity ratings of universal facial expressions of emotion. *Motivation & Emotion*, *22*, 315–327.

Warrier, V., Grasby, K., Uzefovsky, F., Toro, R., Smith, P., Chakrabarti, B., . . . Baron-Cohen, S. (2017). Genome-wide meta-analysis of cognitive empathy: Heritability, and correlates with sex, neuropsychiatric conditions and cognition. *Molecular Psychiatry*, 23(6), 1402–1409. Retrieved 18 July 2017 from http://dx.doi.org/10.1038/mp.2017.122

ABOUT ATMOSPHERE PRESS

Atmosphere Press is an independent full-service publisher for books in genres ranging from nonfiction to fiction to poetry, with a special emphasis on being an author-friendly approach to the challenges of getting a book into the world. Learn more about what we do at atmospherepress.com.

We encourage you to check out some of Atmosphere's latest releases, which are available at Amazon.com and via order from your local bookstore:

To the Next Step: Your Guide from High School and College to the Real World, nonfiction by Kyle Grappone
The George Stories, a novel by Christopher Gould
No Home Like a Raft, poetry by Martin Jon Porter
Mere Being, poetry by Barry D. Amis
The Traveler, a young adult novel by Jennifer Deaver
Mandated Happiness, a novel by Clayton Tucker
The Third Door, a novel by Jim Williams
The Yoga of Strength, a novel by Andrew Marc Rowe
They Are Almost Invisible, poetry by Elizabeth Carmer
Let the Little Birds Sing, a novel by Sandra Fox Murphy
Carpenters and Catapults: A Girls Can Do Anything Book, children's fiction by Carmen Petro
Spots Before Stripes, a novel by Jonathan Kumar
Auroras over Acadia, poetry by Paul Liebow

Channel: How to be a Clear Channel for Inspiration by Listening, Enjoying, and Trusting Your Intuition, nonfiction by Jessica Ang

Gone Fishing: A Girls Can Do Anything Book, children's fiction by Carmen Petro

Owlfred the Owl, a picture book by Caleb Foster

Love Your Vibe: Using the Power of Sound to Take Command of Your Life, nonfiction by Matt Omo

Transcendence, poetry and images by Vincent Bahar Towliat

Leaving the Ladder: An Ex-Corporate Girl's Guide from the Rat Race to Fulfilment, nonfiction by Lynda Bayada

Adrift, poems by Kristy Peloquin

Letting Nicki Go: A Mother's Journey through Her Daughter's Cancer, nonfiction by Bunny Leach

Time Do Not Stop, poems by William Guest

Dear Old Dogs, a novella by Gwen Head

Bello the Cello, a picture book by Dennis Mathew

How Not to Sell: A Sales Survival Guide, nonfiction by Rashad Daoudi

Ghost Sentence, poems by Mary Flanagan

That Scarlett Bacon, a picture book by Mark Johnson

Such a Nice Girl, a novel by Carol St. John

Makani and the Tiki Mikis, a picture book by Kosta Gregory

What Outlives Us, poems by Larry Levy

Winter Park, a novel by Graham Guest

That Beautiful Season, a novel by Sandra Fox Murphy

What I Cannot Abandon, poems by William Guest

Rescripting the Workplace: Producing Miracles with Bosses, Coworkers, and Bad Days, nonfiction by Pam Boyd

ABOUT THE AUTHOR

Tatiana Lukyanova was born in Leningrad, Soviet Union in 1978.

Since early childhood, her primary interest has been understanding how people think and feel and what drives their decisions and behavior. She dreamt of studying psychology, but destiny prepared a different path for her. She ended up focused on physics and mathematics, where through years of ups and downs she has sharpened her analytical skills.

After acquiring a Master of Science degree in Physics, she moved to the Netherlands to proceed with a scientific career. But once again, she realized that humans interest her way more than particles, molecules, electrons, and quarks. That led her away from science to the challenging and intriguing environment of e-commerce.

For many years, Tatiana was responsible for designing and creating solutions for customers of one of the biggest classifieds in the world, part of the eBay Classifieds Group. Successful at creating hyper-productive teams, she started investing more time into coaching for better communication, as well as working more with external partners to deliver crucial business integrations. Given all that experience and a great passion for human psychology, she decided finally to fulfill her dream and formalize her knowledge by earning a Master of Science degree in Communication, Behaviour and Credibility Analysis at Manchester Metropolitan University, which she concluded with research on the correlation of emotional recognition and children's performance at school.

Today, Tatiana is a mother of two grown-up kids, an entrepreneur, a trainer in corporate agile psychology and one of the founders of EQally - emotional intelligence training application. She has decided to share her lifelong learning and experience, backed up by science, and presented in a form that appeals to everyone, with the hope that this awareness will help to build a better world for our children and us.